AN INTRODUCTION

TO

FLY

TYING

AN INTRODUCTION TO

TO

FLY TYING

PETER COCKWILL

Grange BOOKS

A QUANTUM BOOK

Published by Grange Books
An imprint of Grange Books plc
The Grange
Grange Yard
London SE1 3AG

Copyright © 1990 Quintet Publishing Limited

This edition printed 1996

ISBN 1-85627-853-0

This book was produced by
Quantum Books Ltd
6 Blundell Street
London N7 9BH
Printed in China

C O N T E N T S

FOREWORD

Fly fishing as a sport comprises of a number of linked disciplines or skills, all of which should be mastered in order to be both knowledgeable and proficient at the sport.

First we have the skill of casting, the ability to place the fly at the end of the leader exactly where we want it to be, where the fish are. The second is termed water-craft, the ability to read water to know where the fish are lying and how to approach our quarry whether we are fishing fast tumbling rivers or limpid stillwater pools. Also under the term 'water-craft' we have the skills required to manipulate a boat on some of our larger reservoirs, lakes and lochs. The next skill may, at first sight, be a little beyond most beginners, but a little knowledge will go a long way; the understanding of aquatic entomology – the ability to recognize what the trout is feeding on and being able to match a particular insect to a fly in the fly box. Last but not least we have the craft of fly dressing – the ability to create for oneself flies to tempt the trout.

No matter how good a shop-bought fly is, nothing quite compares with the feeling one gets when a trout is caught on a fly of one's own creation. An angler who does not tie his own flies can in no way be described as a complete fly fisherman.

We will never know where fly fishing started and we certainly will never know who the first person was that placed feathers and wool on to a crude fishing hook to tempt the spotted fish that rose to the fluttering insect. All we do know is that man was recorded fishing with a fly in 240 AD by the Roman writer Aelian. The fly was made with red wool and feathers from a cockerel and used on the river Astracus in Macedonia. In those days it was not a sport, but part of man's labour to provide food for his family. There are references to what could be fly fishing in earlier works but they are just passing hints, intriguing but not conclusive, so we will never know who tied the first fly.

Today fly dressing has become a very popular aspect of fly fishing with fly tying guilds and clubs throughout the fishing world. From Iceland to New Zealand and from Eastern Europe to the United States of America there are those that while away the long winter nights at the fly tying vice creating patterns to deceive the next season's fish. As they tie the basic or intricate fly, they are transported in their minds to their favourite waters as fly dressing fuels hopes and creates dreams of catching bigger fish.

Today's angler is extremely lucky for there are many courses at adult education centres or fishing clubs devoted to teaching the craft of fly tying or fly dressing. When I started out there was no such luxury. I had to teach myself from the few books that were available at that time. My first flies defied imagination but over the years they have got slightly better, and I do not mind showing them to people as they actually look like flies now.

A lot of water has flowed beneath the proverbial bridge, a mass of feathers have fluttered to the floor and more hooks than I care to count have been lost in the pile of the carpet since I first tied flies and fished with Peter Cockwill. Suffice to say that the author is one of the best fly fishermen in England today, with a vast knowledge of our sport. Why not join him through the pages of this book, at the various stages of fly tying, and become the complete fly fisherman.

There is no rule to say that a badly tied fly won't catch a fish, but through this book we can strive for perfection in our flies, and as with any skill 'Practice makes Perfect'.

Taff Price

Rainbow perfection, the author with an 18lb 14oz trophy.

INTRODUCTION

My aim in writing this introductory book on the art of fly tying is to put together the elements of the way in which I have taught fly tying to a great many people over the past 20 years and to provide the basis for many more to join the ranks of those who make flies. Men, women, youngsters and the retired and yes, even those with disabilities can all tie flies and find magic in creating a thing of beauty from scraps of feather, fur, thread and tinsel wrapped round a hook.

I have heard many reasons given to explain the desire to tie flies. They include the pure practicalities of wanting to make variations on commercially available patterns so as to achieve a better catch rate; the wish to save money by making one's own; as a way of combining an interesting hobby for the dark evenings with the sport of fly fishing; even to the ambition to tie a perfect fly just as an art form involving intricate hand manipulations.

Every person who makes flies can pitch their skills at any level of proficiency they wish but we all have to start with the basics and this book will set the reader off on the right course: after that it is up to you to decide how far to take it.

A B O V E : A 40lb King Salmon from Alaska which the Author is
about to release after an epic battle.

Fly tying may appear an immensely complex and highly skilled subject when first witnessed at, say, a State Fair or Country Show and I have often heard someone say: 'I would never be able to do such a thing, my hands are too clumsy' or that their eyes were not good enough. I will repeat that anyone who wants to and is taught properly can make flies and I know of men whose work involves the hardest manual labour and whose hands are stiff and badly cracked and yet who make the most exquisite flies and I have taught people with poor eyesight, and those who can barely peel a potato, to make flies which catch fish; the ultimate test of an artificial fly.

One thing for sure, you will always remember the first fish you catch on a fly of your own tying. Large or small, it matters not for the important thing is that the fish saw your fly as an edible item and took it. My first attempts at fly tying were without the aid of a book or any form of instruction and the resultant 'fly' was a bit of a mess but it caught me a trout from a little creek and now, 30 years later, I can still see that flash of gold as the 10 in brownie darted up from the gravel and seized my fly and made my day.

Since that day I have caught many thousands of fish on my own flies, including bluegills in an Oregon desert lake, steelheads in a Washington stream, king salmon in Alaska, brown trout from Ireland and a memorable fish indeed, the once British record rainbow trout at 20 lb 7 oz from Avington Lakes, Hants, but since overtaken by a 21 lb 4 oz fish from Loch Argyll, Scotland.

Fly tying has let me sit at a fly-tying bench alongside such greats as John Veniard and Taff Price and to fish with the legendary Lee Wulff in Africa and Jim Teeny in Oregon, as well as providing many exhilarating experiences beside river and lake which have led to lasting friendships and all with the common bond of the fly tyer.

WHAT IS A FLY?

To a fisherman the art of fly tying embraces not only the representation of actual flies but also a much wider spectrum in that imitations of all manner of aquatic life can be created, including shrimps, small fish, snails and frogs. In fact, anything that a fish might eat can be suggested by the tying of an artificial fly. There are patterns that do not actually represent any living creature but nevertheless they catch fish and because they are created

at the fly tying vice they are called artificial flies.

An understanding of the main groupings of artificial flies will help to make sense of the many patterns in this book and the reasons for their construction. I divide flies into four principal groups, with the first being the nymphs.

NYMPHS Under this group come all the aquatic stages of the many flies which hatch from water and creatures which spend their entire lives underwater, such as the shrimps, hoglouse (cress sows) and water beetles. Flies tied to represent this group are mostly imitative.

DRY FLIES This group includes all the adult insects which emerge from the nymphal stages as well as terrestrial flies which find their way on to water and other land or tree-based insects which fall on to the surface . Again, flies tied to represent this group are mostly imitative although some can be said to be suggestive in that their tying does not imitate the fly but merely suggests it by the appearance of the artificial when seen by a fish below the surface.

STANDARD WETS These are the flies which in reality imitate very little and as their name implies are fished under the surface. They are mostly very old patterns which follow a basically similar format using a wide range of materials, and certainly represent something to the fish but what that is is not clear. But wet flies do catch fish and because they are a challenge to tie well they are essential work for a fly tyer.

LURES These often represent nothing that swims or lives near water because of their size and colour but they also include patterns tied to represent fish, mice, frogs and other creatures which fish eat from time to time. Many lures are often nothing more than larger versions of standard wets. Fish do take lures but whether from territorial or sexual aggression or because they look and act 'edible' we will never know. Suffice to say that fish do take lures. Why a feeding fish that will steadfastly refuse the most carefully tied and fished imitation of the creatures it is feeding on will hurl itself at a large, gaudy lure is a mystery. Virtually all artificial flies fall within these four groups and the techniques shown in this book will enable flies from all of them to be tied.

THE ESSENTIALS

There are some tools which are necessary for fly tying and it is well to become familiar with them from the beginning. At the end of the book I have listed a few additional tools but to begin with there are some that are needed to form the basis of your kit.

THE VICE

The hook has to be held firmly in order to make the operations of fly tying as simple as possible and the easiest way of doing this is is by the use of a purpose-made vice. It is true that some fly-tyers hold the hook in their fingers but I would never presume to teach anyone in that manner as it unnecessarily complicates matters.

Fly tying vices range from the cheap and nasty to wonderful precision tools, but what we require is a functional tool that holds the hook firmly and is not too expensive. For about $15 (£10) there are some super vices imported from Southern Asia which are more than adequate, and are marketed by a variety of tackle outlets. They are essentially of two types which have collet-type jaws operated by a screw or a metal lever on a cam.

A collet is a tapered and divided piece of metal which when drawn backwards through a tube causes the ends to be compressed together so that objects can be grip-

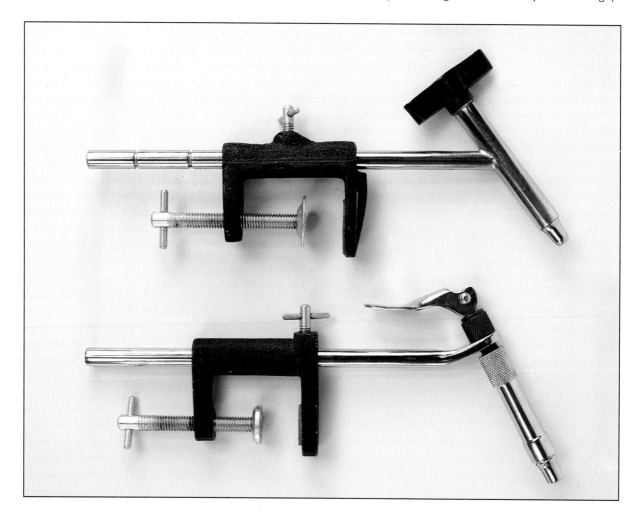

ABOVE:
Collet-style jaws which clamp together as they are pulled back into the vice body.

RIGHT:
Ideal working position.

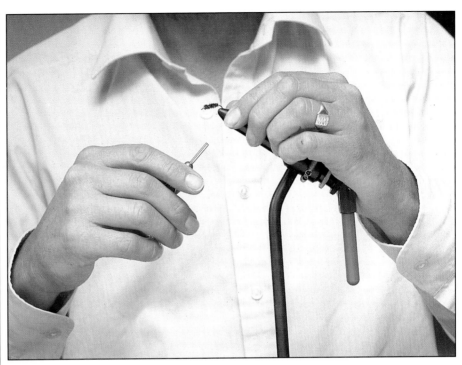

ABOVE: The all essential scissors: here, a cheaper pair for tinsels.

OPPOSITE: Basic vices showing screw and lever action.

ped. A fly-tying vice is made so that the collet ends come together as level jaws to grip the hook securely. Personally I think that the most straightforward system of tightening the collet jaws is with a screw operation as this is more positive than the lever and easier to set. Later, you may find a lever vice to be faster and more efficient.

The shaft of the vice goes into a clamp which can be fixed to a table-top and it is as well to choose a suitable work area where either good natural light falls on to the vice or a suitable artificial light source can be positioned. It is best to have the light coming from above and behind on to the work area. I assume throughout this book that the instructions are for right-handed persons but where applicable I have included special instructions for the left-handed.

Positioning the vice for ease of operation is largely a matter of adjustment to your own personal posture but generally it is best to have the vice just below eye-level when at a seated position and about 10 in in front of your body.

SCISSORS

After the vice — some would say before it — the next most important piece of equipment is a really good pair of scissors. Fly tying involves cutting fine materials with a

ABOVE: A fine pointed pair of scissors for fur and feather.

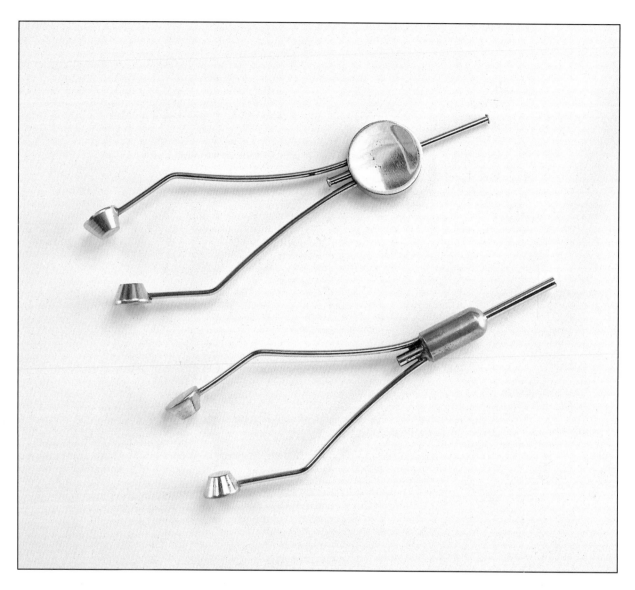

good degree of accuracy and this just cannot be achieved with scissors which are either blunt or which have tips that do not meet properly. Invest in as good a pair as you can afford and look after them by using them to cut fine materials only, NEVER wire or tinsel. It is far better to have another, cheap pair for cutting metal or coarse material. Get into the habit right away of having two pairs and using each for its correct purpose.

The choice of whether to have the scissors with a curve to the tips is yours but do make sure that the tool is not too long, 4 to 6in is about right, and that it is comfortable to use in that the finger holes are big enough and the cutting operation is not stiff. Check before you buy scissors by asking to cut a single feather fibre with the very tip of the blades. You should be able to do so with the absolute minimum of effort.

A B O V E : **Two types of bobbin holder.**

BOBBIN HOLDER

Consider that the whole essence of fly tying involves using a fine thread to tie materials to the hook and you can understand that anything which helps to control accurate placement of the thread will be of enormous benefit. What a bobbin holder does is to grip the spool so that it will only release more thread when just enough of a pull is made to allow the spool to revolve. When allowed to hang from the hook the weight of the holder and the grip of its arms should prevent the spool from turning so that effectively the bobbin holder acts as a tension control for the thread. Also, being fed through a fine tube, the thread can be very accurately placed and if you get into the habit of holding the bobbin in the palm of your hand the tube becomes an extension of your fingers.

There are several different designs of bobbin holder so choose one that you like and which feels comfortable. Problems can occur when a sharp bit inside the tube-lip cuts the thread but the latest type have a ceramic liner which never wears and does not develop a cutting edge. I have used the simple metal ones for years and got through many spools of thread with no problem.

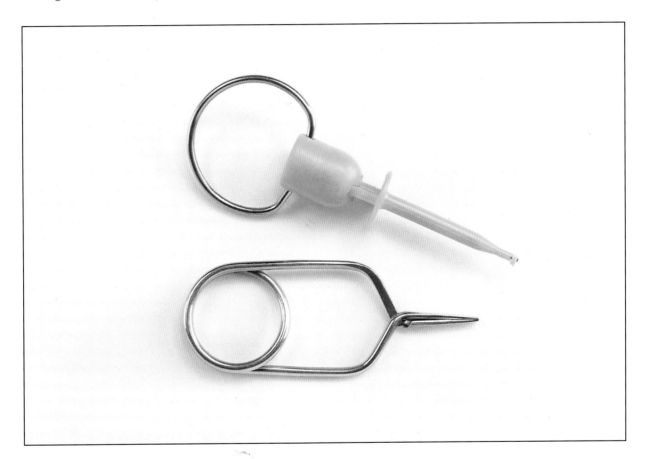

ABOVE: Traditional and Eezi hackle pliers.

HACKLE PLIERS

This is a simple little device which operates like a miniature pair of fixed-jaw pliers to grip small and delicate materials. Mostly used to grip hackles, hackle pliers are a very useful tool and there are several different designs. The conventional type has stood the test of time although I like the Eezi model where a plunger action allows a small piece of wire to grip the hackle. Relatively inexpensive, $1.50 (£1) or so, but an essential tool.

DUBBING NEEDLE

Quite simply a needle set in a handle and apart from its main use of picking out dubbed material bodies it has a host of other uses in fly tying. A dubbing needle will cost less than a pair of hackle pliers, or you can make your own.

BELOW: A dubbing needle.

WHIP-FINISH TOOL

At first sight this looks like one of those fiendishly cunning devices for making a complete idiot out of a beginner. But a well-made fly should be completed with a whip finish to give it strength and although this is possible to produce by hand the whip finish is easy when done with this remarkable tool.

These are all you need in the way of tools to make fly tying as straightforward as possible and when we move on to techniques you will see where each has its place and function. I prefer to keep my tools in a leather wallet where they are safe and always to hand, especially as I do not have the luxury of a permanent fly-tying bench.

BELOW: A whip finish tool.

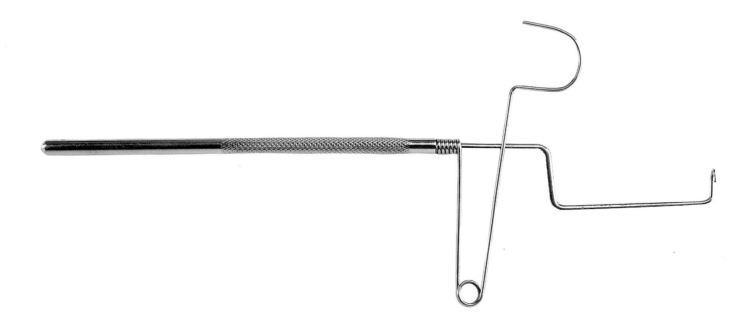

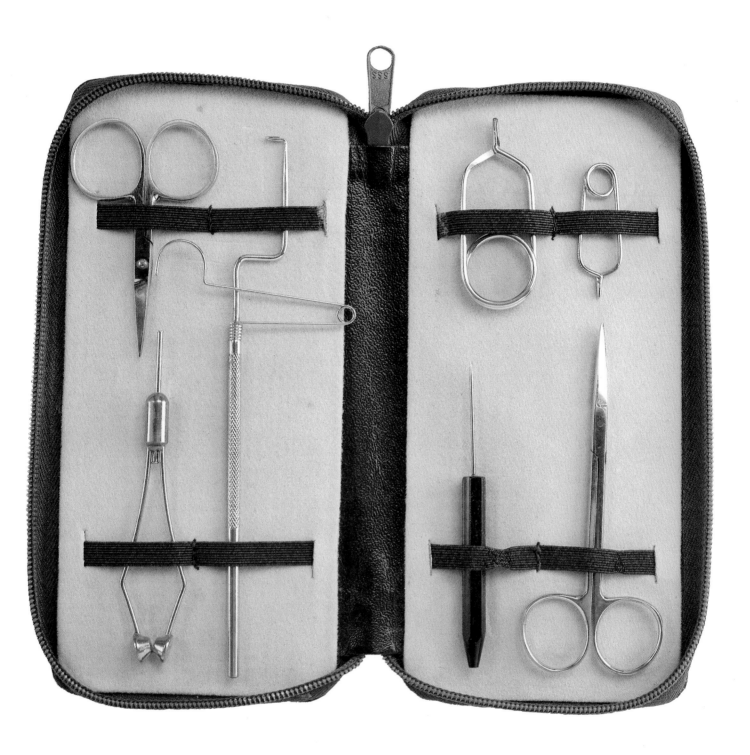

ABOVE: A zipped leather
wallet to contain the basic set
of tools.

MATERIALS

Traditionally, fly tying involves the use of a wide variety of fur and feather with the addition of tinsel in the form of wire or oval or flat section, but today all manner of man-made material is incorporated into fly dressings and almost anything can be used. An understanding of the basic feather and fur requirements will greatly assist you in coming to terms with the various stages in making flies from the four groups I discussed on page 9.

It is possible to buy kits of material which contain lots of different feathers to tie a wide variety of flies, but I prefer to start someone off with a simple selection which enables all the main techniques to be covered and a stock of flies to be acquired without any great initial expense. Many once widely used feathers are now extremely difficult to obtain and indeed it is often illegal to trade in the plumage of certain protected bird species which at one time provided plumage in common usage for a great many patterns.

As anglers and fly-tyers we should be seen to be fully aware of the pressures on the world's wildlife and our interests should not in any way endanger a species.

RIGHT: A magnificent Jungle Cock neck.

LEFT : A selection of
natural coloured necks
(capes).

Where therefore it was once acceptable to use, say, feathers from a jungle fowl we must now use a substitute or feathers from birds reared specifically for the purpose. You might be surprised to learn that many birds are reared to supply the fly-tying market, so great is the continual demand for plumage.

Feathers that fly-tyers use more than any other are hackles from ordinary poultry. These are the neck feathers from the cock and hen birds and there are many colour varieties. Good quality hackles are becoming increasingly scarce and there are not enough naturally occurring necks from free-range birds to supply the world demand. This has led to poultry being reared just for their neck plumage and genetically engineered and bred to provide the perfect hackle. No wonder that such feathers may well be very expensive, but at least they are available.

The well-known Metz hackle from the US is a prime example of perfect feather production for the fly-tying market. Also, too, with the ban on culling young seals there is now very little seal fur available for fly-tying but perfectly acceptable substitutes are available from a variety of commonly occurring fur-bearing animals so that there is no need to use the original material specified for so many patterns. It is no disaster, for the fish cannot tell the difference!

RIGHT : A very high
quality 'genetically' produced
Grizzle neck.

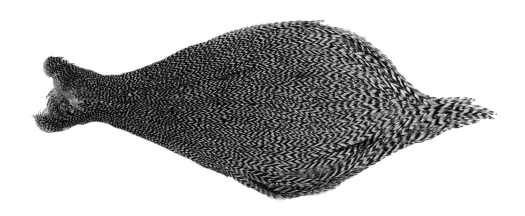

A good basis to begin fly tying includes the following selection of materials in addition to the range of tools already listed:

1. A spool of ready-waxed tying thread
2. A natural brown hen neck
3. A dyed black hen neck
4. A natural red game cock neck
5. A dyed black cock neck
6. A cock pheasant (rooster) centre tail feather
7. A bunch of peacock herl
8. A set of grey mallard flight quills
9. Three packets of seal's fur substitute
10. Three lengths of wool, red, black, fluorescent green
11. Spools of medium width gold and silver tinsel

A B O V E : The necessary basic selection of materials to start fly tying.

12. Spools of fine gold and silver wire

13. A dyed or natural black squirrel tail

This is not a very long or exhaustive list of materials but with it you can tie known patterns which encompass all the techniques described in this book and then add other materials to make up the patterns which you might want to tie. Get the basics right and you can then make any fly.

My suggested starter list of materials as shown opposite may seem strange, so I will discuss each item in turn so that you will begin to understand the terminology of fly tying and some of the reasons for the items listed.

1. Traditionally, fly tying was done with silk thread and, later, cottons and synthetics which were rubbed with a soft wax as the fly was being made. The wax helps the thread to stick to the hook and materials without unravelling as each stage is done. Nowadays we use synthetic threads of incredible strength for their diameter and which are prepared ready-waxed.

2. This is the neck or 'cape' taken from a hen bird and it will have a variety of hackle sizes on it. A plain brown is as useful as any to start with and is cheap. The accompanying photograph shows a complete hen-neck with a large and small hackle from it alongside. Look at the individual feathers (as shown in the photograph opposite) and you will see that a hen feather is wide and rounded and appears soft, while the cock feather is sharp and narrow and looks spiky. Hen feathers are mostly used for flies which will fish under the surface (wet flies). Cock feathers are tied on flies to be fished on the surface (dry flies), their stiffer, spikier fibres enabling the fly to sit on the surface-tension. A similar fly made with hen hackle fibres cannot support itself and will soon sink.

Become familiar with the look and feel of hackles and you will soon be able to differentiate them. A really good quality cock neck would have all the feathers, from the very smallest upwards, of identical coloration and marking. Each feather would be long and slim and very short in the fibre and there would be a high proportion of small hackles. Necks like this are reasonably common in the natural reds but exceedingly rare in colours such as Furnace (red game with black centre and black tips) or Grizzle (black and white barred). A good natural black is also difficult to obtain but one can make excellent dyed black necks by using a natural red as the base colour, for there are plenty available.

3. That is why this one is listed as a dyed black hen as it will be much easier to obtain than a natural one and considerably cheaper. A black hen neck allows many wet flies to be made.

4. Plenty of natural red game necks are of good quality. This feather makes excellent dry flies and is also used as tail whisks. Remember this one, you will use it more than any other.

5. A natural black cock neck is a rare thing but once again the dyed natural red saves the day. An extremely useful feather, a black cock hackle is especially good for dry flies and also for some lure tyings and other functions.

6. Roosters are not so common in the US but in Britain, where the driven bird is the basis of the big estate shoots, the common pheasant is reared in huge numbers. The famous Teeny Nymph is often tied from English feathers as I send many thousands across the Atlantic each year to my friend Jim Teeny. The two centre tail feathers are used to make the Pheasant Tail Nymph which has world-wide appeal as a basic nymph imitator,

B E L O W : A cock neck showing small and large hackle positions.

but the fibres are also used for tails of larger dry flies or when knotted as legs for terrestrials such as the Crane Fly.

7. Where would fly tyers be without the tail plumage of the gorgeous peacock? The bushy, shiny green feathers make excellent chunky bodies when wrapped round a hook and stripped of their flue (the little fibres clinging to the central stem) make a marvellous segmented effect for a dry fly body.

8. Grey mallard flight quills are taken from the common mallard, either male or female, but most common wild ducks provide a grey flight feather. It is the ideal one with which to learn winging for it is a strong feather and holds its individual fibres together very well. The important thing about winging is that you must have a feather from each wing of the bird in order for them to make a pair, much as a left and a right hand make a pair, two lefts do not match up. It is the same with bird feathers. Being flight feathers they have very efficient hook-and-eye systems to hold each fibre together. They therefore hold well when being tied to a hook. An ordinary plumage feather will not have such strong links for each fibre and when you use, say, bronze mallard and summer duck the feather has very weak fibre links and is therefore much harder to use as a winging medium.

9. A seal's fur substitute will allow dubbing to be learnt. There is no better way to create a shaggy body effect on a fly to give an illusion of bulk, and at the same time allow light to pass through, than when using individual hairs trapped by turns of thread. Olive, brown and black will allow several different patterns to be made and form the basis of a collection of dubbing materials.

10. Wool can be used to form tails, tags of bodies on flies and all sorts of colours can be used. The three suggested will enable you to make a lot of very effective patterns.

11. Medium-width tinsel allows for bodies to be made which reflect lots of light and many standard wet flies use tinsel bodies. Learn to use tinsel properly and very smart flies can be tied.

12. Wire makes an excellent ribbing material on a fly body both to give strength and weight to the pattern and to supply the all-important segmented effect which is attractive to a trout. Look at most insects and you will see that they are segmented. Copy this and your fly begins to look lifelike.

13. Wings made of hair are very common on artificial

B E L O W : The very clear difference between a cock and hen hackle.

flies and there is a separate technique for applying it. Squirrel tails are easy to use and very common and a natural or dyed black will enable you to make many patterns.

Once you use these materials you will be fascinated, and begin the process of becoming a dedicated fly fisher. It will not be long before other materials get added, some of which will be used on a regular basis and others which will be there just in case or because they look good. The original storage box overflows into a series of boxes, and then into a proper chest of drawers and then a roomful! Scavenging of odd bits of material from friends' houses begins and you start to acquire a reputation as the strange, ghoul-like person who stops to retrieve bits from animals and birds killed on the highway. It is all good fun and part of the mystique.

PROPORTIONS

The most common theme in my method of teaching fly tying is continually to emphasise the need to get the dressing of a fly put together in the correct proportions, by which is meant the relative length of, say, the hackle and tail to the size of hook being used and the insect or creature being imitated. It is true that greatly exaggerating the size of one portion of a fly will sometimes enhance its attractiveness to a fish but usually it is better to keep all the elements of the dressing in proportion.

Referring again to the four principal groups of flies it is fairly easy to prepare a representative diagram of each and indicate the correct proportions.

Starting off with group 1, the nymphs, this is a diagram of a typical nymph dressing. It is shown alongside a drawing of a natural Ephemerid nymph and I hope that you see the similarity. Of course, the copy does not resemble the real insect but the proportions are right:

(a) The natural insect has a segmented abdomen, almost always seven segments, and the artificial should suggest this with its ribbing of the abdomen.

(b) The natural has its abdomen about twice as long as the thorax — look at the artificial!

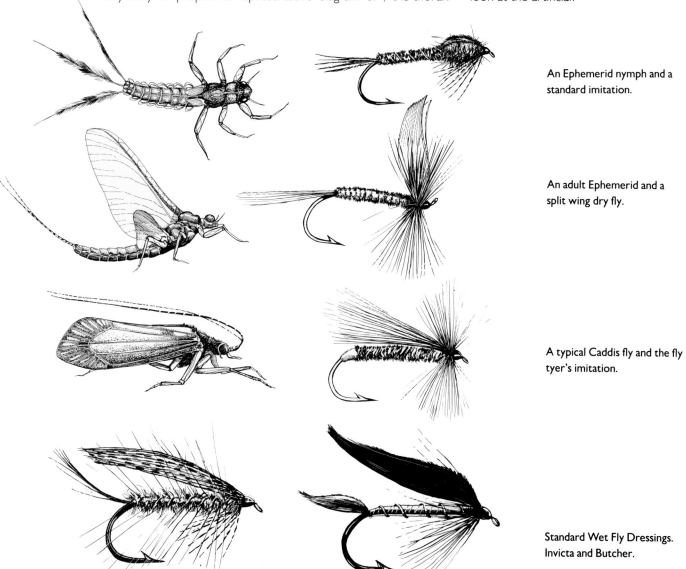

An Ephemerid nymph and a standard imitation.

An adult Ephemerid and a split wing dry fly.

A typical Caddis fly and the fly tyer's imitation.

Standard Wet Fly Dressings. Invicta and Butcher.

(c) The natural has a tail roughly the length of the abdomen and its legs are also the same length. The fibres we use to suggest the tail and legs therefore need to be in proportion.

(d) The natural has a distinct hump to its thorax, this is where the embryo wings are housed. Our imitation has the same pronounced hump.

Moving on to group 2, I have shown a typical upwing adult Ephemerid against the fly tyer's suggestion and a roof-winged caddis fly against its artificial. Look at the segmentation, length of wings, angle of wings, thickness of body and length of legs, and the absence or presence of tail. All are in proportion to the natural creature.

Group 3 is slightly more difficult to explain because here we are not imitating any specific form of life but suggesting by virtue of colour and form that the artificial we have created appears edible. There are, however, certain ground-rules with regard to proportions on standard wets that if adhered to will make the fly not only very attractive to look at from our human, aesthetic point of view but also appealing to the fish.

The diagram shows two typical standard wet fly dressings. Notice how certain elements of the artificial are kept in proportion to a natural insect even though this type of fly rarely actually imitates one. The ribbing of the abdomen again shows seven segments. The tail, wing and hackle lengths are relative to a natural, so once again we are working on correct proportions. Finally, to group 4, the lures.

Most flies in this category represent nothing but, as has been said earlier, they are often little more than enlarged standard wets and again therefore the same standards of proportion apply. Look at the drawing of a typical hair-wing lure and you can see immediately the same proportioning as the standard wet.

A streamer pattern or Matuka follows much the same idea but enlarges one element, in this case the wing length.

A Muddler originally intended to imitate a minnow (in Europe Phoxinus; in the US a number of small baitfish), so a drawing of the Muddler and the original minnow shows just how far away from the original theme some Muddler patterns now are. And they all of them catch fish!

Lures with mobile tails, called leeches in the US, and Nobblers in the UK, rely on a very long tail of soft material, either man-made or natural, to give the lure a

A typical Hair Wing Lure.

matuka style.

Don Gapen's original Muddler Minnow and the fish it suggests.

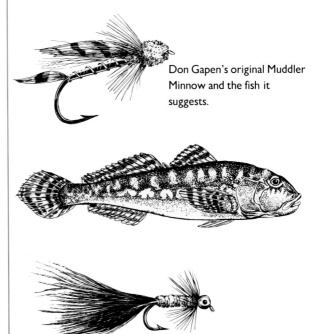

A leech or nobbler type of lure.

wriggling, pulsating movement when retrieved. A brilliant imitation of a black leech, but what does a magenta pattern suggest? Goodness knows, but at times the fish will impale themselves on it. Even a wiggle-tail fly has to have the correct proportions or it will not work properly when retrieved. A 2 in tail pulses; a 4-in one wiggles. When we move on to actual techniques I shall continually refer to the need to get the correct proportions, so read back over this section. It is very important.

HOOKS

Without a hook we have little chance of catching a fish and there are now hundreds of different hook patterns all based on a pointed, bent and barbed length of wire. Modern fly tying is done with an eyed hook either straight, up or down-eyed depending on personal preference for the type of fly being tied. The length of the shank can vary tremendously as can the gape of the hook and the set of the point. Hooks come either plain or forged, the latter having the bend compressed to give it more strength. The modern trend in fly fishing is to use barbless hooks so that an unwanted fish can be released with the minimum injury and so provide future sport. However, the vast majority of fly hooks are barbed and a range of commonly used patterns is shown.

Hooks are tempered in that the metal is heat-treated to harden it, but tempering is an absolute science for the hook must not be so brittle that it breaks when under tension, i.e. when in the mouth of a fish, and nor must it be so soft that it straightens out under a pull.

If as a fly tyer you are going to spend a considerable amount of time constructing a fly on a hook then the first thing you should do is to test its temper. If you do not, then your own temper is likely to be very severely tested if after much effort and time the hook breaks or straightens on the first fish it hooks. However, testing a hook takes but a moment and you do it as soon as the hook is placed in the vice.

At this point you will learn how to place a hook correctly into a fly-tying vice. The object is to cover the point of the hook with the jaws of the vice so that the tying thread does not catch on the sharp point and cut it. The hook must also be held so that the shank is level to make the tying operation easier and you do this by getting a good hold with the vice jaws on the lower part of the bend. Do not screw up the vice jaws so tight that the face of the jaws can be damaged, use just enough grip to ensure that the hook is firmly held.

The temper-testing operation is not too technical, all you do is to depress the hook end with your thumb and let it go. If the hook bends or breaks discard it and try another. Ideally, it should return instantly to its original shape with a 'ping'.

The old adage that you get the best by paying the most applies very much to hooks but even then you will get the occasional bad one in a batch.

ABOVE: A wide selection of the many hook patterns available.

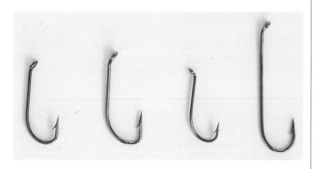

ABOVE: The basic selection of hooks, size 12 sproat down eye, size 10 limerick down eye, size 12 sproat up eye, size 10 perfect long shank.

Fly tyers have an enormous range of patterns from which to choose and there is a pattern for every conceivable fly within the different patterns made by Eagle Claw of the US, Mustad of Norway and Partridge of England.

To start fly tying I suggest that you obtain a packet of 25 each of the following hooks:
Size 12 Sproat bend standard-length shank, down eye.
Size 10 Limerick bend standard-shank length, down eye.
Size 12 Sproat bend standard-shank length, up eye.
Size 10 Perfect bend long-shank, down eye.

With this selection you can tie nymphs, dry flies, standard wets and lures and then, later on, you can make other flies on patterns of your own selection or based on the recommendation of the tyer who originated the fly you want to make.

Look after your hooks by keeping them dry: corrosion is a terrible thing for fishing hooks and has been the cause of many a lost fish. A small compartmented plastic box makes an ideal storage container, with the advantage that the hook types are readily seen. Make sure that the lid fits securely, for one day you will drop your hook box and it is not much fun picking them out of the carpet and sorting out several hundred different hooks into sizes and patterns. It teaches you all about hooks, but what a way to learn!

With a little knowledge of hooks and one of a suitable temper in the vice now is the time to move to the first proper stage of becoming a fly tyer.

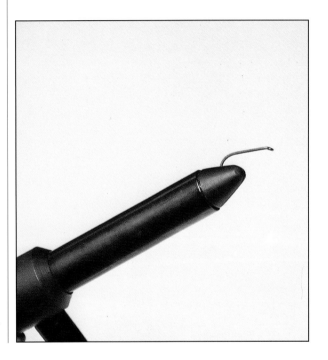

A B O V E : The correct position of a hook in the vice.

L E F T : How to test a hook for 'temper'.

TECHNIQUES

Here comes the difficult stuff! How do you get all those little bits of feather, thread and tinsel on to a half-inch-long hook and make it look like a fly worth putting on the end of your line? Remember what Taff Price said in his Foreword about his first flies being absolutely dreadful and how I said the same thing in the Introduction about my own early efforts?

You now have the benefit of both mine and Taff's experience and the fact that we have tied many thousands of flies and taught each other – and a great many other people – how to share this super hobby of fly tying.

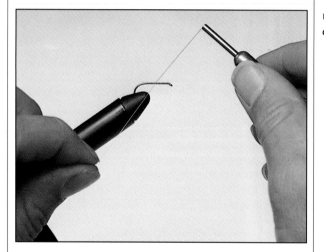

LEFT: Tying thread crossed over the shank.

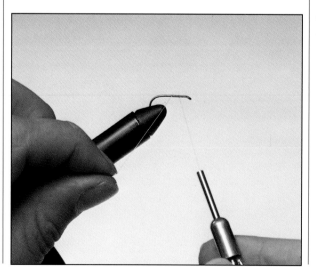

LEFT: Four turns of thread towards the eye.

Take a Size 10 standard-shank hook and put it in the vice. We are going to learn how to start and finish the fly before any material is applied to the hook.

Most books on fly tying tell you to lay the thread on to the hook-shank in touching turns from the eye to the bend. However, other than for very fine tying I have never believed in doing this and all I want to teach you is how to make flies to fish with. If you want to go on to perfection of technique later on then that is the subject of another book. Now we are going to tie flies.

With the bobbin held in the right hand and about 4-in of thread protruding from the bobbin, take hold of the end of the thread with the left hand and place your hand at the lower axis of the vice as shown in the photographs opposite and below.

Lay the thread on to the hook shank roughly midway and take four even turns round the shank, going away from the body and working towards the hook eye.

R I G H T : Four turns back to the bend and the thread is attached.

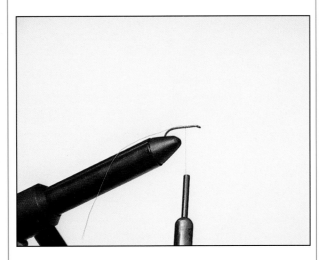

R I G H T : Hand whip finish.

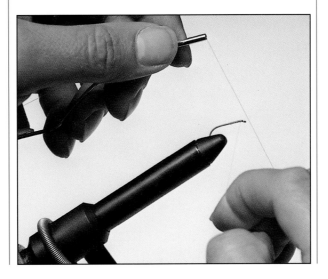

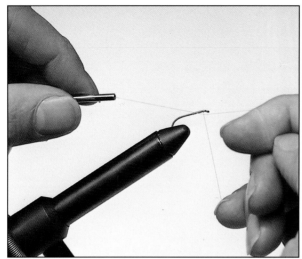

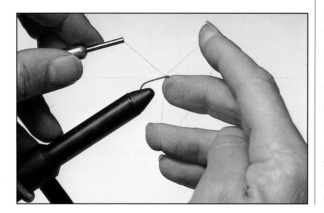

Stop and then take four more turns going back down towards the bend so that you cover the previous four turns. Now you can let go of the thread in the left hand and allow the bobbin to hang down below the hook and the thread will stay in place. That's it, the first stage is over: you have the thread on the hook.

Next, take the thread down towards the bend and back up towards the eye, not necessarily to form a base for the dressing but more to get the hang of holding the bobbin and using the end of the tube as though it is your fingers to get very accurate placement of the thread. Take off the thread and do the whole thing again and end up with the bobbin hanging off the hook just down from the eye.

Cut off the waste end and run the tying thread up to the hook eye. Having started the fly we are now going to finish it. It might seem odd but the hardest thing you will learn is how to finish a fly properly. It is no good having got to the stage of completing the dressing of a fly and then finding out that you do not know how to finish it off! Learn the whip finish technique and you will have no further problems with fly tying. There are two ways of doing a whip finish, one is with your hands and the other is with a tool. At first, both seem impossible but if you follow these instructions and refer constantly to the photographs you will have no problems.

T O P : With a clockwise rotation of your hand and using the forefinger as a lead you trap the thread from the bobbin against the hook shank with the loop in your fingers.

A B O V E : Still using the forefinger to maintain loop tension, the other two fingers now press on to the bark thread of the loop so as to turn the thread around the shank.

R I G H T : The loop is now brought down below the hook with all three fingers, now moving to press on what is the front thread of the loop. The forefinger again takes the lead to bring the loop of thread up over the hook once more.

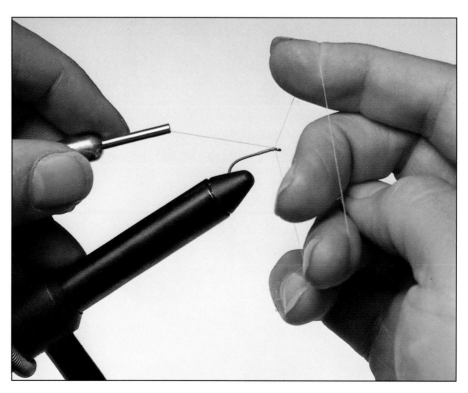

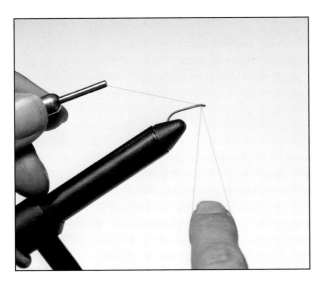

LEFT: When four or five turns have been wrapped around the shank, the loop is brought down below the hook and just the forefinger and thumb can pinch the remains of the loop until it is pulled tight.

RIGHT: Pull the bobbin gently and the loop will be pulled towards the hook shank until the forefinger and thumb can pinch the remains of the loop until it is pulled through.

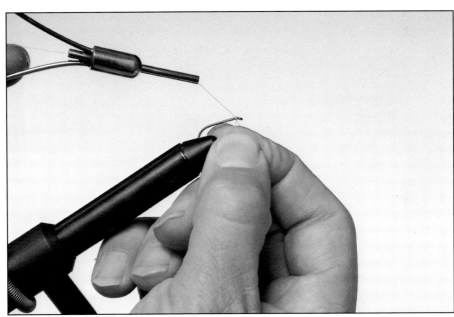

BELOW: Alternatively, you can use the dubbing needle to control the loop being pulled in tight.

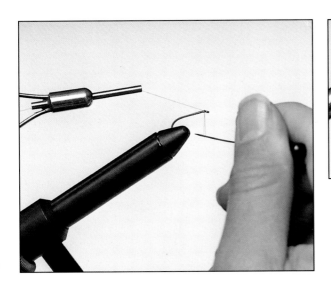

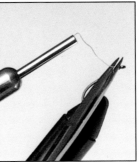

LEFT: Scissors cut off the thread and the completed whip finish is the most secure way to finish off a fly.

THE WHIP FINISH TOOL

I do not know who the American was who invented this twisted bit of metal but he must have been a genius. But you must learn how to use the tool properly. I recall one fly-tying class where I decided to teach the whip finish instead of the hand method I had previously taught. But I had never actually used a whip finish tool, rashly assuming that it would be easy. I felt somewhat foolish having to admit defeat and go away to learn the technique before the next class!

The tool has two loops, one large and one small. Make sure that the bobbin has released about 10 in of thread and hold it in the left hand at the base of the vice stem. With the tool in the right hand you now place it behind the thread and engage the large and small hooks in the thread as shown. Now move the left hand up so that it is level with the tool and at all times maintain tension on the thread, not too much but just enough to keep it taut.

Bring your right hand up so that the tool is horizontal and begin to turn it in a clockwise direction towards the hook. The thread coming from the hook and held by the small loop will now touch the thread being held by the bobbin in the left hand and a simple figure 4 appears.

BELOW: Engage large and small loops of tool from behind thread.

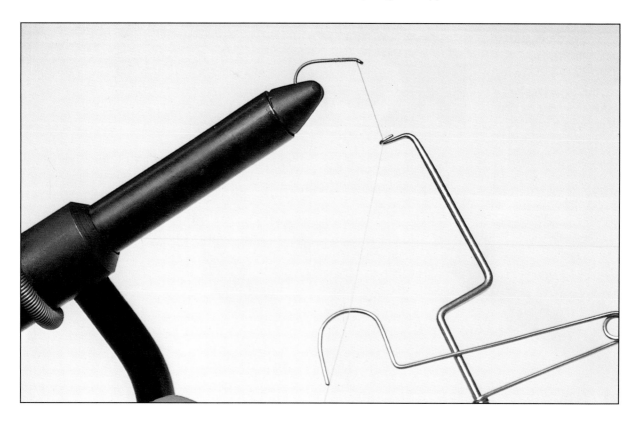

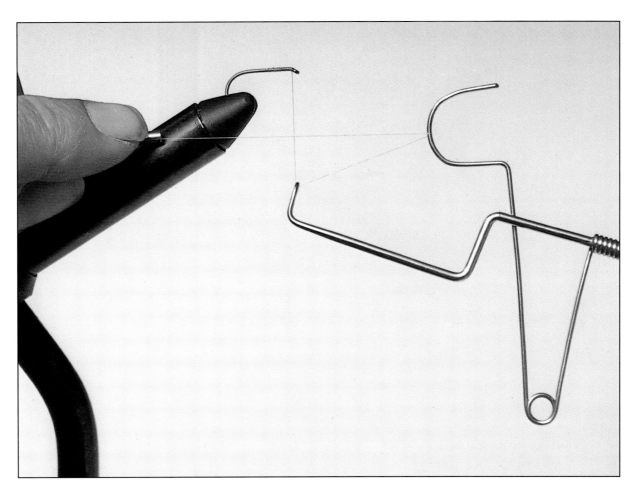

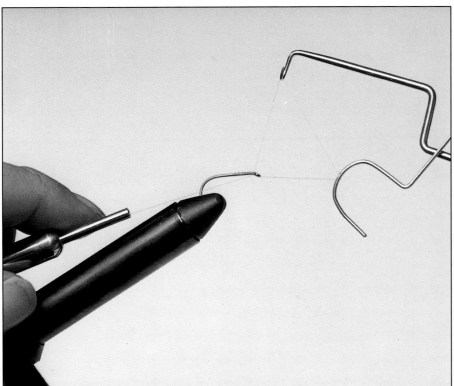

ABOVE: Rotate tool clockwise while raising it to horizontal so that the figure 4 is formed with the thread.

LEFT: Continue to rotate clockwise until loop of thread controlled by small loop of tool traps thread from bobbin against hook shank.

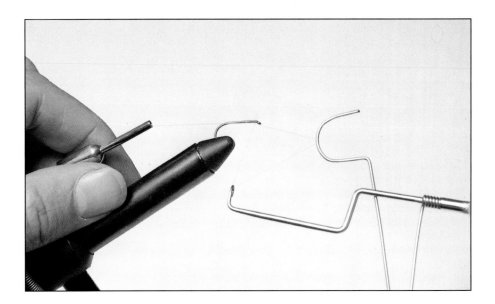

RIGHT: Turn the tool around the hook while also rotating it clockwise so that samll loop always has bend facing the hook.

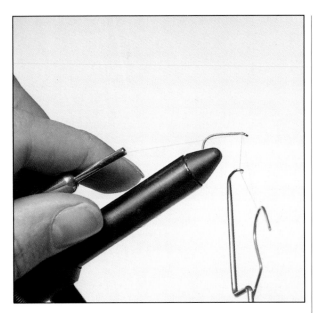

ABOVE: After four or five turns bring tool down under hook and at right angles to it.

You must now concentrate on the thread being controlled by the small loop of the tool. Continue to rotate the tool clockwise so that it becomes trapped against the hook shank. The left hand can rise during this process until it is level with the hook. You should now be at the situation shown in photograph (x). The small loop is now controlling the process and in order to get it to wrap the thread round the hook shank and so round itself it is now necessary to turn to tool round the hook and at the same time slowly rotate it in the same clockwise direction so that at all times the bend of the little loop faces directly toward the hook. Fail to do that and the thread will disengage from the loop.

Do about five turns round the hook shank and then bring the tool down under the hook so that the thread is now at right-angles to the shank. It is nearly all over!

Slip the small loop off the thread so that it is now only held by the large loop. If you now gently pull to the left with the left hand the loop of thread being held by the large loop of the tool will be drawn in towards the hook. When the tool butts up against the hook you disengage the large loop and pull tight with the left hand. That's it, you have now completed a whip finish. Properly tied with waxed synthetic thread a whip finish is strong enough to last the life of the fly without further protection, but it is usual to cover the thread with varnish to seal it and give a smooth finish.

The whip finish is by far the best way to complete a fly and much more secure than a series of half-hitches. Take the trouble to learn it and you will save time and money in the long term as well as having a well-tied fly.

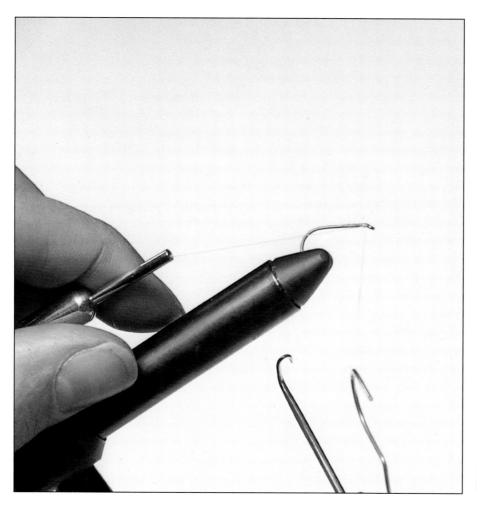

LEFT: Disengage small loop of tool.

RIGHT: Pull gently on bobbin so that large loop of tool is pulled up to the hook shank then disengage it.

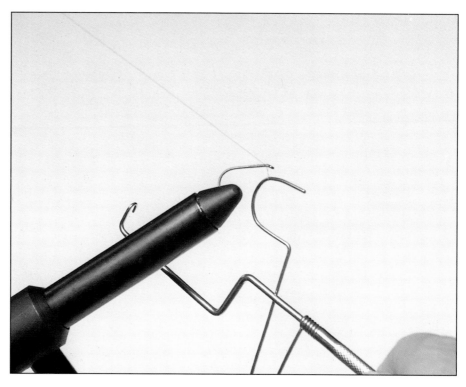

Wild brown trout from Lough Melvin in Ireland.

MAKING YOUR FIRST FLY

Get to the stage of a hook held securely in the vice and the tying thread secured to the hook shank. We will start off with a pattern made from feather fibre for the body. It is better to start by doing this as you immediately get used to handling feather rather than strong wool. Take two fibres of peacock herl and cut off the curly end where the fibre was attached to the main quill and then line up the two cut ends in your left hand so that about half an in of material projects from between your finger and thumb. Offer this up at an angle to the hook and just touching it.

LEFT: Prepare the peacock herl for tying in.

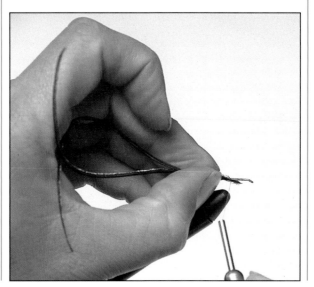

LEFT: Tie the herls to the hook shank.

Holding the bobbin in your right hand raise it up and round the hook and all the time maintain tension on the thread. As the thread comes up round the hook shank it will cross the ends of the two sections of peacock herl and trap them against the hook. Carry on round the hook shank with the thread and twice more wrap it round the peacock fibres. You will always be turning the thread over the hook away from your body in a clockwise motion.

Having secured the body material to the hook the usual step would be to take the tying thread up towards the eye of the hook and then wrap the body material round the shank. Peacock fibre is, however, rather a fragile material and the first fish caught on the fly will invariably cut one of the fibres with its teeth. Consequently, the fibre will then unravel and very shortly you have no fly.

R I G H T : Herls and tying thread held together.

R I G H T : Winding on the body and the twist develops.

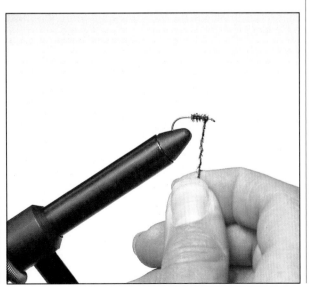

ABOVE: A correctly proportioned body with room left for the pattern being tied.

We are now going to strengthen the body material of this fly by taking the two fibres of herl into the right hand along with the tying thread and commence winding them all round the hook shank, working first down towards the bend and then back up towards the eye so as to build up a nice, chunky body. After about the fourth turn round the hook you will notice that the herls are twisting and that the thread is twisted with them. As you wrap this twist round the hook, each herl is being trapped by the other and by the thread, so if the herl should become cut it cannot unravel because it is trapped by so many turns. This is the way to get a good, strong fly which will last for more than one fish.

At this juncture I am going to stress the first of the points about proportioning.

It is vital that as you attach each piece of material to the hook you take note of how it will appear at the final stage. For example, even with such a seemingly simple operation as attaching two strands of peacock herl and making a body, it is important that the body starts and finishes at defined points on the shank of the hook. There is only going to be a herl body on this fly, so the twist should be taken down to the bend of the hook to fill the level section of shank. It should finish at the end with sufficient room left to make a hackle and a whip finish.

Probably, the most common mistake you will make is to leave insufficient room at the head of the fly; this not only makes it very difficult to finish the fly but it appears very crude and introduces a weak point where it can become undone.

A correctly constructed and proportioned fly not only catches fish more efficiently but it 'looks' right. You will soon be like every other fly tyer: when a fellow angler looks in your box and asks where you buy your flies you will look smug and say 'Actually, I make my own!'. So now we have a well-tied body of peacock herl on the hook and if we add a hackle the fly will be born and usable.

For this, our first-ever fly, it is going to be a wet fly that will be fished underwater and therefore the hackle to use is one from a hen neck. It will easily absorb water and sink, whereas a cock hackle would be all stiff and spiky and prevent the fly from penetrating the surface film.

Use a dyed black hen hackle and the fly will be a recognised pattern called a Black and Peacock Spider, a

R I G H T : Selecting a
hackle of the right fibre length
for the pattern being tied.

A B O V E : How to remove
a hackle from a cape.

R I G H T : Removing the
fluff from the base of the
hackle prior to tying in.

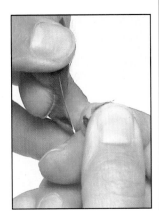

very effective artificial. Look at your black hen neck and
you will see that at the base, which is the top of the
bird's head, the hackles are short and have short fibres,
while those at the other end of the neck are much
longer and have correspondingly longer fibres.

A hackle must be selected that will have the correct
fibre length for the size of fly being tied. Proportioning
again!

Refer to the drawings of a standard wet fly and you
will see that the hackle fibre length is slightly longer than
the total shank length. Therefore we need a hackle with
fibres of these proportions for the hook in the vice.
Instead of randomly taking a hackle off the neck and
finding that it is not right it is better to offer the whole
neck up to the hook and bend out individual hackles
until you have one that is right and then pluck it off the
neck. Do this by gripping the hackle at its base and
pulling it towards the base of the neck, away from its
natural growth line, and it will pop out of the skin.

The hackle must now be prepared before it can be
tied to the hook and this involves stripping off the downy
fluff from either side of the base of the stem so that
only the actual fibres proper are left. Do this by gripping
the fluff each side of the stem and pulling down and
away from the stem.

L E F T : Attaching the hackle to the hook shank.

T O P : The natural curve of the feather shows the correct way to tie it in.

A B O V E : The wrong way to tie in a hackle.

Now hold the prepared hackle up between finger and thumb and you will see that it has a distinct curvature and a face side which is on the outside of the curve. If the hackle is tied to the hook and wound so that the curve points towards the eye, the fibres will all slope that way and the fly will look unnatural and oppose the water as it is retrieved, rather than envelop it by curving over the hook.

Correctly positioning the hackle before attaching it to the hook overcomes this problem and it is a matter of offering the prepared hackle up to the hook so that its face is towards you and the natural curve of the feather is over the top of the hook. Look at the photograph above and it is very clear.

Now trap the hackle stem against the hook shank in the same way as you did the peacock herl stems. The tying thread should be on the hook-eye side of the hackle at this point.

This is where we introduce another tool, the hackle pliers. They act like a spare pair of hands and grip the end of the hackle very firmly. Hold them in line with the stem of the hackle and grip the last quarter-inch.

Now wind the hackle round the hook shank in the same direction as the tying thread, i.e. over the body going away from you and in a clockwise direction. Do not twist the hackle but keep its face side pointing at the hook and eye and make each turn at the same place on the shank. Do not let it wander about to cover a long area, keep it compact.

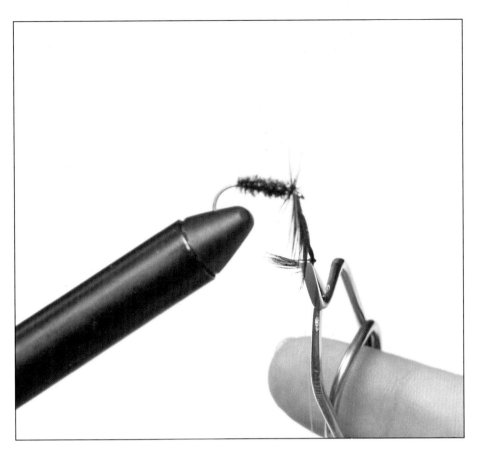

L E F T :
Winding the hackle with the
aid of hackle pliers.

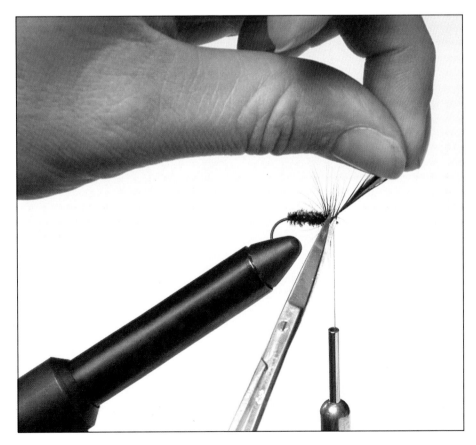

R I G H T : Cutting off the
waste tip of the hackle.

RIGHT : The inevitable odd bits of feather fibre projecting at all angles.

BELOW : Using thumb and first two fingers to stroke back the odd bits of fibre.

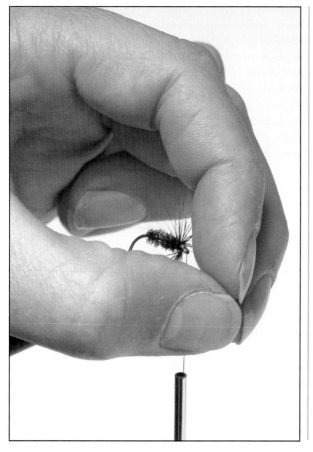

Do about four turns of the hackle and now finish with the hackle pointing down from the shank. Cross it over in front of the tying thread and lift the thread up and over the hook to trap the end of the hackle against the hook. Do a couple of turns over the hackle and you can now carefully cut it off. Use your best scissors and snip the stem close to the hook, but be careful you do not cut the thread as well.

The fly is now virtually complete but before you do the whip finish, which you learnt in a previous section, you will need to tidy up the head of the fly because there are almost always a few odd bits of hackle fibre sticking out at the wrong angle, making the whip finish difficult to carry out.

I tidy up by touching the tips of my thumb and first two fingers of my left hand together, leaving a small gap between them. Then slip this finger/thumb pinch over the eye of the fly and slide it backwards down the body of the fly. Bits of fibre will be stroked backwards, allowing you to take a couple of turns of the thread over this last section to trap them in a backward-sloping profile and leave the way clear for the whip finish.

That is it, your first fly! Now go out and catch a fish on it.

A final professional effect can be created be applying a coating of dope to the whipping. There are several proprietary products for this final stage, some take the form of a varnish which sets like rock and is called head cement. The kind of dope used by model-aircraft makers is perfectly all right for the job and if you apply it with the point of the dubbing needle it will go on very evenly and accurately. Try putting on a layer of black dope and when it is dry add a layer of clear. This gives a shiny head to the fly just like those commercial patterns.

You have now learned to make a simple fly and can put on a herl body and a wet fly hackle, so now it is time to move on to another stage.

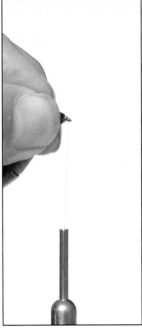

ABOVE: The completed head of a neat fly.

LEFT: Varnishing the whip finish.

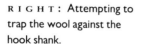

R I G H T : Attempting to trap the wool against the hook shank.

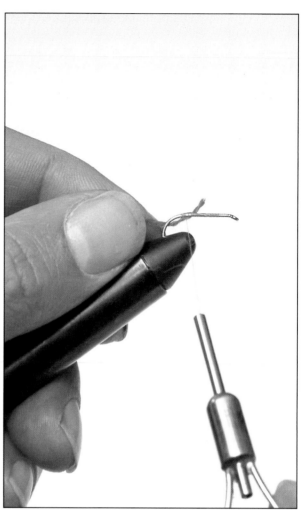

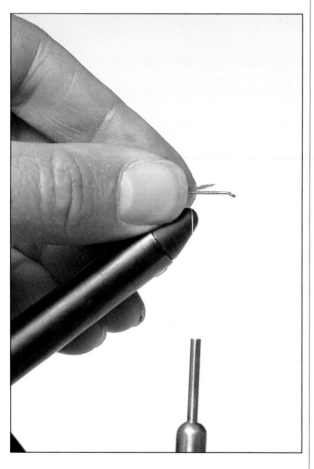

A B O V E : Tying thread at the correct position prior to tying in the tail by pinch and loop.

THE PINCH AND LOOP

This is a technique used to get a piece of material to sit exactly square on the hook shank and it must be mastered or you will never be able to do winging. We are going to start by using the pinch and loop technique to put a wool tail on to a fly.

Try cutting off a section of red wool, an inch will do, and then tying it to the hook shank so that it sits exactly on top of the shank and faces backwards as a tail.

So far we have applied a few bits of herl to the hook and then wound over them to make a body. Try tying the wool tag in the same way by offering it up to the hook and bringing the thread up over it to trap it to the hook. What happens is that the thread pushes the wool round the hook and no matter how quick you do it the wool ends up at an offset angle to the hook and not symmetrical as it should be to make a nice effect and to get the fly to move through the water properly.

The pinch and loop technique will solve this problem and enable you to tie material on to the body of a fly exactly where you want it. First, you need to decide where the tail is to be tied in. It seems obvious — it should be at the end of the fly, but what it means is that the tying thread should be at the point where you want to tie the tail and not still part way up the hook shank. So, having attached the thread to the hook you must now run it down towards the bend of the hook and stop just where the hook starts to bend.

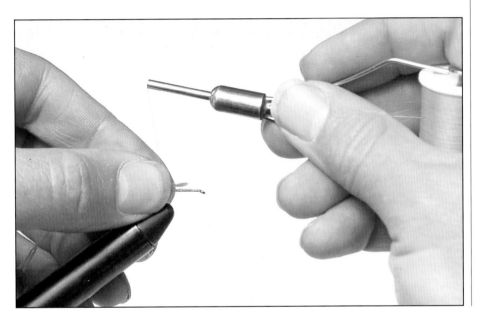

LEFT: Bring the thread up between the hook shank and the thumb.

RIGHT: Loop the thread over the top of the hook and the wool tail and down between finger and hook shank.

Now, hold the piece of wool between the finger and thumb of your left hand and offer it up to the hook so that the wool is lying level with the hook and on top of the shank as in the photograph on page 44, left. Lift the tying thread up so that it slides between the thumb and the wool. Bring the bobbin over the top of the hook and back down the other side so that the thread now slides between the finger and the wool. Now pinch the lot together and if you slacken off the tension on the thread from the bobbin nothing will come loose as it is all being held by the pinch of finger and thumb, which now has a loop of thread going up over the section of wool. Hence the term pinch and loop.

If you now hold the bobbin below the hook shank and pull downwards while still keeping pressure on the

ABOVE: With everything firmly pinched pull down the loop to trap the tail.

LEFT: Trimming the wool tail off to length.

pinch, the loop will slide down between your finger and thumb and trap the wool against the shank of the hook. Do the loop operation again without moving your fingers other than slightly to relax the pinch and again pull tight. Now, if you remove your finger and thumb you will see that the wool is square on top of the hook and exactly positioned to be the tail of your fly.

You can now trim it to length, repeat the operation done on the first pattern and apply a body of peacock herl. Make sure that the turns of herl-twist butt up exactly to the tail where it is tied on and do not overlap it, twisting the tail off-centre. Complete the fly by putting on a hackle from the natural brown hen neck and you now have a wet Red Tag. This is a very famous old trout fly which is also excellent for catching grayling.

BELOW: Herl body butted up exactly to where the tail is tied in.

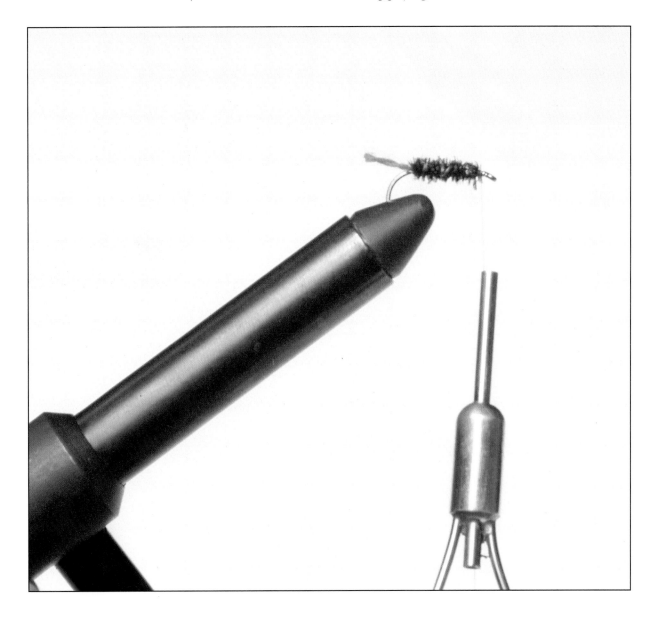

RIBBING

Remember how in the section on proportions I emphasised the importance of the segmented effect in fly tying? You can achieve this by ribbing the body of a fly dressing with a thread or tinsel and no matter whether you are making an exact imitation dry, a simple nymph or a large lure it is always best to aim for the natural look of segmentation and go for six to seven sections in the body. In due course you can gradually increase the width of space between each ribbing turn to more exactly copy nature. It is surprising how much better your fly will look when correctly ribbed.

Let us tie a fly with a rib based on the work we have already mastered.

Start off with pulling a tail of bright green or fluorescent wool and then cut off a 3 in length of silver wire, tying it in by one end so that the long end projects back like a very long tail. Do not just catch the very end of the wire but get at least half the hook shank to tie the wire to so that it is securely trapped. Now make the peacock herl body just as you did before and ensure that sufficient room is left at the head of the fly, because we now have to tie in a piece of wire as well as the hackle.

ABOVE: A length of wire ribbing tied in.

RIGHT: Ribbing up the body.

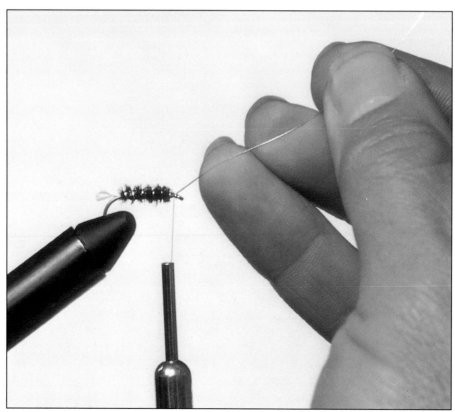

RIGHT: The finished fly 'a mini Viva'.

BELOW: Tie off the ribbing.

With the body complete you now leave the bobbin holder hanging from the eye end of the hook and grasp the wire between thumb and forefinger of your right hand (using the hackle pliers if preferred).

Instead of winding the wire up the hook shank in the same direction as in every other operation you must now wind it anti-clockwise round the hook. This is done so that it will cross the body material in the opposite direction to the way in which it had previously been tied. Not only will it (the ribbing) further strengthen the body, it will also stand out as a rib rather than be hidden by sliding between the turns of body material. This is particularly important when using thick and bushy body material which would otherwise obscure the rib and lessen its impact on the dressing of the fly involved.

Having now run the wire up towards the eye of the fly with the spacing as even as possible, you can you now take the bobbin holder in the left hand and put a couple of turns of thread over the wire to secure it in place. It will sometimes try to unravel itself as it has been wound against the normal pattern of tying, i.e. anti-clockwise instead of clockwise, so it is wise to turn the wire back over the top of the hook shank and bend it back towards the tail section and tie over it again. This produces a double lock to ensure that it does not unravel.

You can now cut off the waste end of the ribbing wire and proceed to add a hackle. If you put on a black hen hackle you will have tied a mini-lure.

A black fly with a green tail is often deadly for trout but I have no idea what it represents to that fish. Already, then, we have made a Black and Peacock Spider, a wet Red Tag and a small lure, often referred to as a Viva.

By using various combinations of the materials in the basic kit you can make a number of well-known patterns all of which you could use with confidence.

TINSEL BODY

This stage will introduce a new element into our fly dressing repertoire in that neatness of tying will now be rather more important than before. We are going to make a standard wet fly which has a body of flat tinsel and to get that to look first-class it is necessary to think carefully about the final effect.

Ideally, the fly should look like the one in the photograph. The tinsel body starts exactly where the tail of the fly is tied in and then runs in a smooth, even way to the hackle. Unless the bed over which the tinsel is to lie is itself flat then the tinsel has no chance. If you make any kind of step in the body the tinsel will have to follow that contour and spoil the overall effect. The hungry trout will not notice it, but good tying techniques at this stage will make life much easier for you later on.

With this fly we will try another material and make the tail from feather fibre.

Pick a hackle from the end of the neck which has the long-fibred feathers. Use the red game cock neck as this will have nice, straight fibres to the hackle and make a neat tail.

ABOVE: An uneven bunch of fibres plucked away from a hackle.

If we want to make a good fly, it will look so much better if the fibrès of the tail all line up at their tips, and this is the way of ensuring that they do.

If you hold the hackle in your right hand, face towards you, and grasp about half an inch section of fibres on the left side of the feather with your left hand and pluck them down and away from the stem of the feather you will see that the tips are all uneven. It would be very difficult to try to line them up now, so discard that feather. Now hold the tip of the hackle in your right hand and run your left thumb and forefinger down the spine of the hackle.

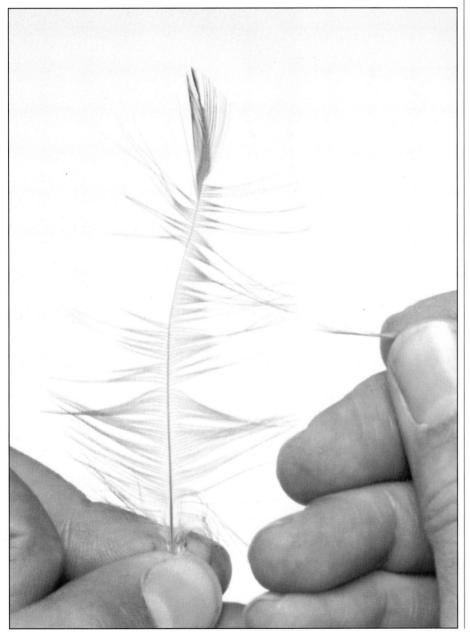

L E F T : Stroking the hackle fibres will let the section plucked away have the tips of equal length.

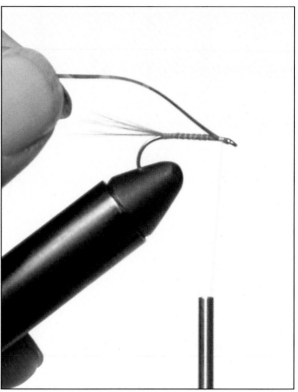

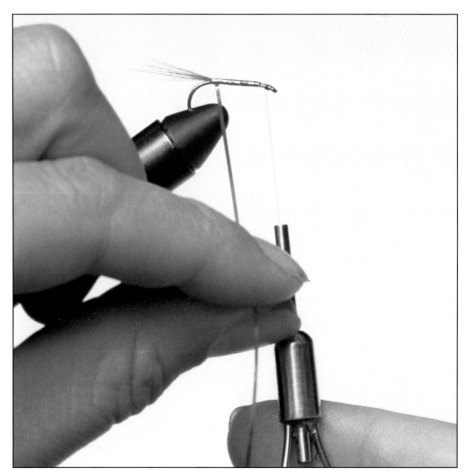

A B O V E , L E F T :
Fibres of cock hackle tied in
for a tail.

A B O V E , R I G H T :
Tie in the tinsel for the body.

R I G H T : Run the tinsel
down to the tail roots.

This will have the effect of making the individual fibres stand out at right-angles from the spine of the feather. You might have to stroke it a couple of times to make them all line up properly. Now take another half inch section of fibres between the thumb and forefinger of your left hand and pluck them away from the centre spine of the feather. You will find that all the tips now line up.

This little bunch of fibres can now be offered up to the hook and tied in with a pinch and loop so that about a length equal to the shank of the hook will project back from the tying-in point. Running along the back of the hook shank will be the remainder of the bunch of fibres. Cut them off at the point level with where the tinsel body will end up near the eye of the hook. Now take turns of tying thread up the hook shank towards the eye and tie down these ends of fibre.

Cut a 3-in length from the spool of flat gold tinsel and tie in one end as in the photograph opposite, right, with the long end projecting back towards the tail. Hold the tinsel again either in finger and thumb or with the aid of

the hackle pliers and wind it down in roughly touching turns towards the tail. When you get to the tail it is most important that the last turn of tinsel exactly touches against the tail fibres. Not just short of them, so that turns of thread show, and neither just over the tail so that it is forced off its position on top of the hook shank and immediately prior to where the bend begins.

Now you can run the tinsel back up towards the eye of the fly, again in roughly touching turns, and then tie it off just as you would a hackle end. You will now have a perfectly smooth, flat tinsel body running from the tail to near the eye. All that remains is to tie-in a hackle from the natural red hen neck and finish off the fly. You now have a simple wet Wickham's Fancy. This is a very old pattern and effective for many species of game fish.

If you wish to make the artificial stronger you could add a gold wire rib and run it up the body in an anti-clockwise spiral, but make sure that when you tie it in the end of the wire rib is tied down level with where the tinsel body is going to finish or you will be introducing a step in the body which will spoil its looks.

ABOVE: Back up towards the head to show the lovely flat effect.

RIGHT: A hen hackle finishes off the tinsel bodied fly.

PALMERING

This is a technique in which the hackle is wound along the body of the fly to give it more bulk and a lifelike effect. It is not difficult to master because you have already learnt how to tie in and wind a hackle.

To make a simple fly such as a Palmered Wickham's, which is a super dry pattern, we will need to start off as in the previous pattern and put on a tail of hackle fibres from the cock cape and then before winding up to the eye of the hook you must tie in a length of gold wire to form the ribbing. Tie it so that as you wind towards the eye you are covering the wire all the way and then there will be no step in the body. Tie in a length of flat gold tinsel and as before wind it down to the tail root and over the wire before winding back up to the eye and tying off.

Now select a feather from the cock red game neck which has the correct fibre length for the hook gape, i.e. just longer than the actual gape. Trim the base of the feather and then stroke the fibres down from then tip towards the base so that they stick out at right-angles from the stem. This makes it easier to wind the hackle for the palmering stage. What you should now have is a

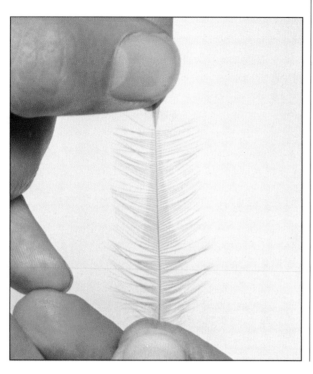

ABOVE: Preparing a hackle for palmering.

RIGHT: Tie in the hackle, the ribbing material is ready at the tail.

length of wire projecting from the tail of the fly and a hackle at the head held by its root.

Grip the hackle tip with the hackle pliers and take a couple of turns round the head as though you are doing a normal hackle and then wind it down towards the tail of the fly in open turns. Do this carefully, keeping the hackle straight and being careful not to twist as you wind.

When you get to the last turn immediately before the tail, you leave the hackle pliers on and hanging down from the hook. Now take hold of the wire, either in your finger and thumb or with a second pair of hackle pliers, and wind it anti-clockwise up the body towards the eye just as you did for the previous ribbing exercise. Make sure that the fibres of the hackle do not get trapped by the wire as you wind, only the hackle stem should be crossed by the turns of wire.

You can use the dubbing needle at this stage and flick the fibres free from the wire as you wind. When the wire gets to the head of the fly, tie it off just as you did the ribbing and end with a whip finish. You can now carefully cut off the stem of the hackle where it is held by the pliers and you have tied your first palmered fly. Congratulations!

ABOVE: The hackle wound down towards the tail to show palmering.

LEFT: The ribbing traps the final turn of the hackle and crosses it all the way up the body.

RIGHT : Offering up the bunch of hackle fibres which will make the 'false' hackle.

FALSE HACKLE

Tying-in a false hackle is a prelude to making a winged standard wet fly but at this point we are discussing variations on a theme as you can already tie thread to a hook, do a whip finish, attach materials, wind a hackle, do a pinch and loop and make a rib.

Refer to the previous section and put on a tail of feather fibre and a body of flat gold tinsel; then turn the hook upside down in the vice so that it is the same as in the photograph.

Now prepare another long-fibred hackle from the red game cock neck and take a rather larger bunch of fibres than you used for the tail. These are going to be the hackle and will be tied in on what is the underneath of the hook shank to fill the gape of the hook just as a fully wound hackle would, except that we are only using some fibres and hence the hackle is a false one. The reason why we do this will soon become apparent.

Offer up the bunch of hackle fibres so that the ends project to just beyond the hook bend and then tie in the bunch with a pinch and loop so that it sits exactly on what will be the underneath of the hook shank. Carefully trim off the waste ends and turn the hook the right way up in the vice.

Look at the upper surface of the hook shank and you will see that it is flat and level with the tinsel body. Had we wound a full hackle and then tried to bring the fibres down underneath the hook shank, by tying over those on the upper surface, there would inevitably have been a bump at this point, which would seriously hinder the next operation, which is that of winging a wet fly.

L E F T : The 'false' hackle tied in.

WINGING

This is where your careful learning of the pinch and loop technique really comes into its own and it is the only way you are going to get wings on to this fly.

First, select a pair of similar-sized wing quills from the grey mallard set. It can be seen from the photograph below, left, that the two mirror-image feathers make a pair. We take a slip of fibre from each quill and put them together to form the wing for the fly.

Selecting the width of a slip of fibre might seem difficult but a rough rule is to make the width about half the hook gape. You can use the dubbing needle to

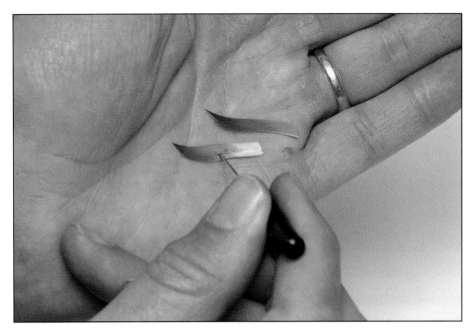

OPPOSITE, LEFT:
A pair of grey mallard wing quills.

OPPOSITE, RIGHT:
A slip of feather removed to make a wing and showing its natural curve.

separate the individual fibres so that the section of fibres you want is clear from the rest, then cut it clear from the feather shaft. Take another section of fibres from the same place on the shaft of the other feather in the pair and now you have two wing slips ready for tying in.

You will quickly realise that you can cut out a section of the fibre without having to be too accurate in gauging its width. If you now look at the two wing slips you will see that each has a curve to it and that if you line up the tips and make them into a pair you will find that when held one way round the natural curve of the slips makes the tips of the pair separate, and held together the other way the natural curve holds them together. It is this latter position we want for a wet fly pattern, while the former is used for split-wing dry flies. These are discussed in the next section.

Already you will have discovered how tricky it is to get the two wing slips to line up exactly level with each other and how it is all too easy to spoil them while attempting it. Here is another very useful piece of advice.

Pick up the wing slip with the curve which when laid in the palm of your left hand will sit with its two ends up in the air. Now put the other slip on your hand so that it is the other way round so that its ends are touching your skin. Take the dubbing needle in the right hand and carefully pierce the second wing slip in its middle. Lift up the needle and the wing slip will stay on it.

Very carefully place this over the top of the other slip and then press the needle point down until the second

ABOVE, TOP: How to pick up wing slips with a dubbing needle.

ABOVE: The two wing slips perfectly matched and ready to be tied in.

slip is also pinned through. You can now lift up the needle and the two wing slips will be exactly positioned together. Grasp them with the finger and thumb of your left hand and there is your first pair of wing slips ready for tying in.

The next stages are explained as clearly as possible and you must note every instruction carefully or the wing of your fly will never sit properly. Ideally, we want it to be on the top of the hook shank and exactly in line with it and also set low so that there is very little gap between wing and hook. The photographs show the perfect set for wet-fly wings and achieving this is entirely dependent on how you use the pinch and loop to put the wings on.

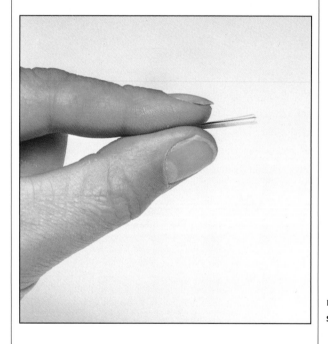

L E F T : Finger and thumb straight to show the pinch.

First, take a look at the photographs of my fingers and you will see that above I have a finger and thumb straight-jointed and that where they pinch together there is a vee-shaped gap towards their tips. If you now look at the photograph opposite, left, where I have bent the finger and thumb joint you will see that the pinch has now moved farther towards the tips. I call this 'increasing the angle of the pinch'. The next photographs show the line between the pinched finger and thumb and if you know that the wing slips will be in this pinch, and hence in this line, then wherever the line of the pinch is seen that will be the line along which the wing will sit when tied down.

If you set the pinch at an offset angle to the hook

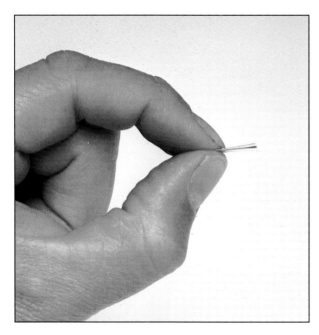

A B O V E , L E F T : Bend the joints and the length of pinch changes.

A B O V E , R I G H T : The line of pinch between the finger and thumb determines exactly where the wing will lie.

shank then the wing will also be at an offset angle. This is the most common fault in winging and one that is seldom understood. The line of the pinch must be exactly above and absolutely in line with the hook shank. Please read through this last section again and make absolutely sure that you understand it.

Now, with the prepared pair of wing slips between finger and thumb of your right hand you must offer the wings up to the hook shank and position them so that the tips project to just beyond the bend of the hook and that they lie parallel with the hook shank and exactly on top of it. Now grip the slips with your left thumb and finger.

Lift the tying thread up between thumb and wing slips, loop it over the top and then down between finger and the slips. Increase the angle of the pitch by bending the joint of the finger and thumb and at the same time ensure that the line of pinch is exactly on top of the hook and dead in line with the shank.

Pull down with the bobbin and the loop of tying thread should now slide down between your pinched finger and thumb and press the wing-tip down on to the hook. You will see the root ends of the slip kick up in the air as they are caught up by the thread.

Without relaxing your pinch, repeat the process to put another turn of thread over the slips and then remove your pinch. Hopefully you will now see your first-ever wing sitting proudly to attention.

Assuming that the wing looks pretty good you now

take it in a pinch again and put a couple of turns of thread round the base of the slips to secure them, and then while still holding the pinch get your best scissors and cut off the waste ends. If you cut off the ends without holding the wings you risk pushing them off-centre, because you cannot cut with exactly equal force on each blade of the scissors. All that now remains is to do a whip finish and the fly is complete. Congratulations, you now have a wet Wickham's Fancy!

The ability to make a winged wet fly that is correctly proportioned and with the wing absolutely on top and in line with the hook shank is one of the fundamental assessments of an accomplished fly tier.

ABOVE, TOP LEFT: The pair of wings offered up to the hook and the tying thread in the correct position.

ABOVE, TOP RIGHT: The loop pulled down between the pinch and the end fibres kicked up.

ABOVE, LEFT: Holding the wing in order to cut off the waste fibres.

ABOVE, RIGHT: The completed winged wet fly.

DRY FLY WINGS

At this point, refer to the chapter on proportioning and look at the length of wing slips on a typical dry fly and the hackle fibre length as well as the way the whole fly is constructed. There are several ways to make a dry fly and I believe that the following method will quickly get you into making perfectly acceptable patterns.

Take a dry fly hook, the up-eyed one, and put it in the vice. In fact, there is very little to choose between up- or down-eyed hooks for efficiency of use in dry-fly fishing but there is no doubt that a dry fly does look better tied on an up-eyed hook.

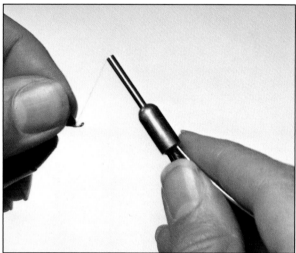

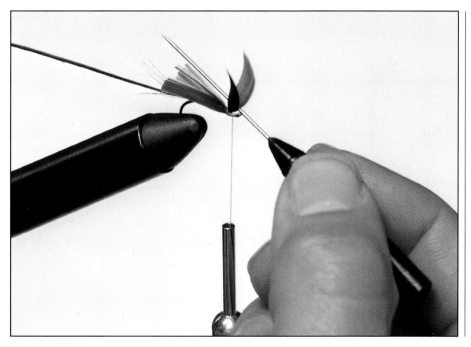

ABOVE, LEFT: Wing slips offered up in the reverse position for a dry fly.

ABOVE, RIGHT: Lift up the slips and take two turns of thread at their base.

LEFT: Separate the slips with a dubbing needle.

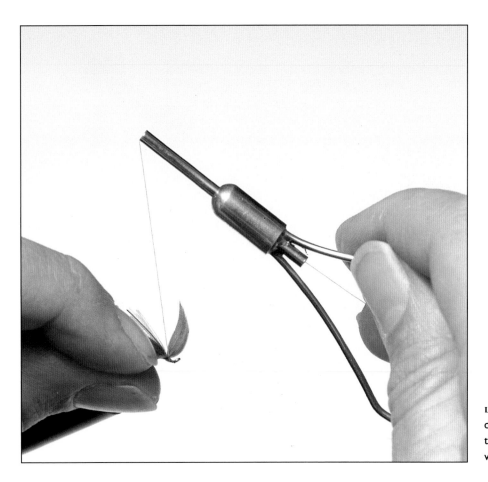

LEFT: Pull one wing slip down and take a turn of thread between the wing slips.

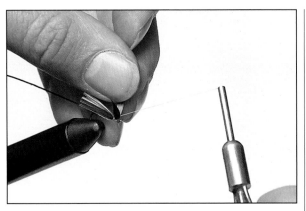

ABOVE: A turn of thread from the opposite direction between the wing slips.

Run-on tying thread, take it down to the bend and attach a few cock hackle fibres with a pinch and loop, a technique which should have become routine. We are going to make a quill-bodied fly which can successfully imitate many of the adult up-winged flies and at the same time acquire another tying and handling technique.

Material required for the body is the familiar section of peacock herl, but this time stripped of its flue. Get these off the stem by pulling the piece between finger and thumb with the nail of the thumb pressing on to the stem, which effectively rubs the fibres off. It will be necessary to do this a few times to ensure that you get a clean de-fuzzed stem.

Look at the piece of peacock quill and you will see that it has a light and a dark side, so that when wound along the hook shank it will give a segmented effect.

Tie in the piece of prepared peacock quill at its thinner end and just where the tail of the fly is tied off leave it projecting over the end of the fly. Now run the tying thread up to about a third of the shank length from the eye of the hook. Do not take it too close because a lot of work has yet to be done.

A B O V E : Cut off the wing roots at an angle.

Now prepare another pair of wing slips from the mallard quills, but this time when you put them together to make a pair you will do so in a way that allows the natural curve of each slip of feather to curve away from the other. The tips of the slips will now be separated.

Take the pair of slips and reverse them so that they now appear to be back-to-front for tying in. The tips should be projecting over the eye of the hook rather than down towards the bend as in wet-fly tying. Offer the two slips up to the hook and ensure that the length of the wing will be correctly proportioned when tied in, i.e. about one-and-a-half times the hook gape.

Perform the same operation as for tying-in the wing slips on a wet fly and when you have done, use the pinch and loop securing turn of thread, release the pinch and make another turn over the roots of the slips; this time it will be down towards the bend of the hook and not towards the eye.

At this point you must ignore the supposed fragility of feather fibres. With your left hand hold the wing slips and bend them backwards towards the bend of the hook. Take the tying thread and make two turns round

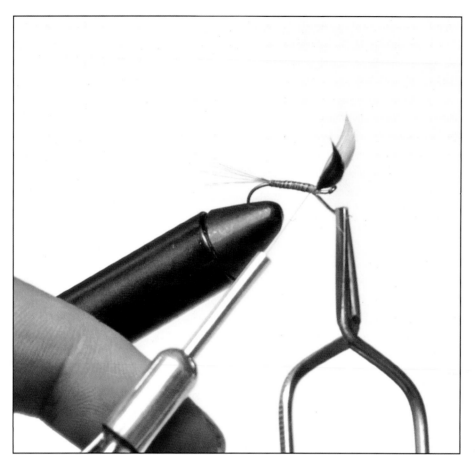

L E F T : Wind up the
stripped quill body.

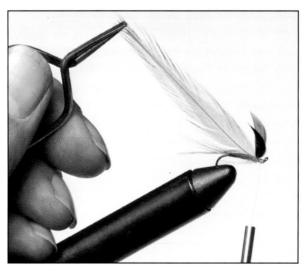

A B O V E : Tie in a cock
hackle.

the hook shank immediately next to the slips on the
eye-side of them so that they will now be held upright.
The two slips will probably have stuck together while
you did this, so separate them, very carefully by inserting
the tip of the dubbing needle between the two slips to
press them apart.

Now take the nearest one in your left hand and bend
it away from the other so that you can bring the tying
thread up between the two slips and to the rear of
them. Let go of the wing slip and take a locking turn
round the hook at the rear of the slips. Now take the
other wing slip, the one farthest away from you, and
again bend it away from the hook.

Bring the tying thread up between the slips, this time
you will be coming from the rear, and again take a
locking turn round the hook and in front of the slips. It
sounds rather complex, but what you now have is the
two wing slips firmly tied on in an upright position and
separated by a criss-cross of threads. They are now
perfectly safe and cannot be affected by any other
operation. It is far better when tying a dry fly pattern to
get the winging bit over at an early stage.

Now it is time to cut off the wing roots, but here it pays to be crafty and cut them at an angle so that the ends actually taper back towards the end of the hook. This makes it much easier to form the body of the fly because there is no step in it. Take a few turns of tying thread over the wing-roots to make them into a neat taper. Tie off against the hook shank and return the tying thread to the actual wing base.

Take the end of the quill between finger and thumb and in touching turns run it up towards the wing base and tie it off. That makes the body of the fly. It now only remains to tie in the hackle. It should not be too difficult, you have done it several times before.

Prepare a suitable red game cock hackle, its fibre length a little more than the gape of the hook, and tie it in by its base. Grip the end with the hackle pliers and take two turns round the hook shank on the eyed side of the wings. Now run the hackle under the hook shank and take two more turns round the hook at the rear of the wings so that they end up looking as if they are surrounded by hackle fibres. You can generally finish by doing a few more turns of the hackle at the eye side of the wings before tying off and completing a whip finish.

BELOW : Wind on the cock hackle either side of the wings.

As the hackle fibres should be sticking out at right-angles from the hook all round the eye area, you might find it better to pull the hackle fibres out of the way over the body of the fly while you do the whip finish. It is amazing what you can do with the dry fly once those wings have been put firmly in their place.

As has been said earlier there are several different ways of tying dry fly wings and with different materials, but this is a classic way and by now you must wonder what all the mystique is about dry flies.

HAIR WING

Hair is a very different material from feathers, for although it is constructed from the same base, keratin, it is not compressible. Unlike feather fibre, it is difficult to get a firm grip on hair with tying thread and we therefore need to use a different technique when tying it in. Some hair is easy because it is hollow, but most hair, and the type we are using, is made of a solid shaft. Running through a simple lure tying we can use the long-shank hook as the starting base and make a larger version of the Viva we made earlier in this book.

BELOW: A squirrel tail with the hair pulled at right angles to the bone to even up the tips.

ABOVE: Pulling the short hairs from the section of hair to be used as a wing.

First, tie in a length of the fluorescent green wool to act as a tail and then a 3-in section of flat silver tinsel and a similar length of black wool. Make sure that you tie in so that the body can be bound over a level bed. Run the black wool up towards the eye and tie off when it is about three-quarters of the way up the shank, and then follow up with silver tinsel on the opposite spiral. Cut off the waste ends and then tie-in a false hackle of long black cock fibres. This now leaves the way clear to tie in the hair wing.

It is time to become familiar with the black squirrel tail. It is very much like a feather in construction in that it has a central stem, the bone with the fibres coming off at an angle. If you stroke the fibres away from the bone and in a downward direction you can again line up the tips just like we did with the hackle fibres.

RIGHT: Offer the hair wing up for length.

Do this with a section of the hair, a bunch about as thick as a Biro refill will do, and then cut it free from the bone. If we were now to tie in this section of hair it would almost certainly come loose at some time because the long hairs would not be firmly enough gripped by the tying thread. The reason for this is that with the long hairs, known as guard hairs, is the under-fur which is a much softer, shorter-fibre hair. Tie it all in together and you will find that the longer guard hairs are not gripped firmly enough and work loose.

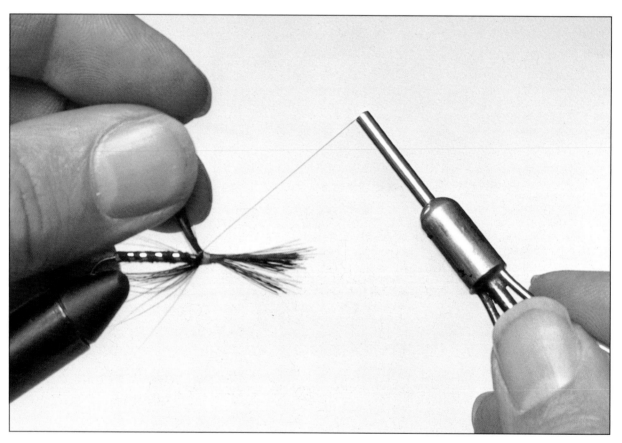

ABOVE: Lift up the wing to take a locking turn around it.

What has to be done is to remove the under-fur and this is easily accomplished by holding the section of hair by its tips and gently pulling the under-fur free from it. You will be surprised how much comes away.

In the right hand, the prepared hair wing can now be offered up to the hook and its length adjusted so that its tips come to just beyond the bend of the hook. Now you can tie it in with the pinch and loop.

It is quite a lot easier to tie in these feather fibre wings but once you have got the hair bunch on the tip of the hook with a few turns of thread it now needs to be locked into position. This is done by lifting up the hair wing in the left hand and passing the thread over the top and then back underneath the hair before then pulling backwards towards the eye of the hook. It has the effect of compressing the bunch of hair together and lifting it up clear of the hook shank.

Take a few turns of thread over the hair and, working towards the bend of the hook, go over this locking turn of thread and again press down the wing so that it is closer to the hook shank. The locking turn of thread is buried under these other turns and the whole wing is secure. Now you can hold it firmly in your left hand and cut off the waste ends with a taper so that when you do the tidying-up turns of thread and the whip finish it will all make a smooth fly.

Add a few coats of black varnish or dope and then a clear coat and you have a very smart lure.

BELOW: Press down the wing and tie over the locking turn.

BELOW, LEFT: Cut off the waste ends of the hair wing.

BELOW, RIGHT: A whip finish on a hair wing shows its much larger bulk.

RIGHT: Pheasant tail
fibres tied in for the tail.

BELOW: The abdomen
wound two-thirds up the
shank.

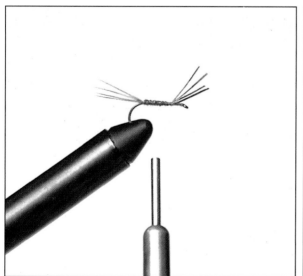

PHEASANT TAIL

Flies made from pheasant tail fibres account for huge
numbers of fish every year and what would we fly tyers
do if the bird was no longer reared for sport
shooting?

A nymph made from pheasant tail fibres will simulate
most larval stages of aquatic insects and as a fly fisher
you should certainly never be without one in your box.

We will make a classic pheasant tail nymph, so put a
standard-shank hook in the vice, attach the thread and
run it down to the bend of the hook. The pheasant tail
feather is much like any other in that its fibres are at an
angle to the main shaft, but it is very much longer and
thicker.

Pull the three or four fibres with which to make the tail away from the main stem at right-angles so that the tips line up. I often use four fibres instead of three. Most nymphs have three tails but trout cannot count so if you put four on, the fly will last longer as it is usually the tails that get chewed up.

The first thing to do , then, is to tie in the tail so that the fibres are the correct length without having to spoil the whole effect of the fly by cutting them to length later on. Proportioning again! Make just the pinch and loop turns of thread to secure the fibres to the hook and then lift the remainder up away from the hook to leave the hook shank free to tie in a length of gold wire, which you must leave projecting back over the tail. Run the tying thread up the hook shank to about two-thirds of its length and then wind the pheasant tail fibres up from the tail to the thread and tie them off.

BELOW : Bending back the fibres and tying over them.

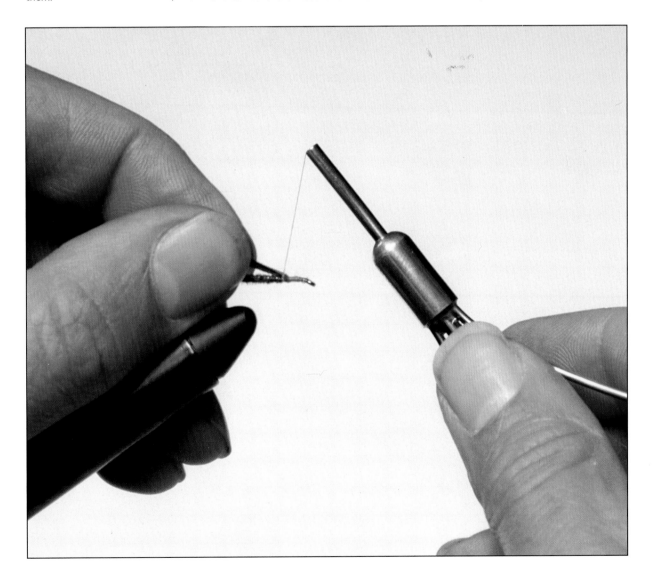

Tie them off, but do not cut them off because we have more use for them. Now you can spiral up the gold wire in the opposite direction and again remember about proportioning, doing about six turns so that segmentation is simulated.

Tie off and cut the gold wire. The next part is very important if you want to achieve a good-looking fly. It entails bending the remainder of the pheasant tail fibres back towards the tail of the fly and taking turns of thread over them so that they are tied down to the point where the body actually finishes. Fail to do this and you get a gap between abdomen and thorax which looks terrible.

Still using pheasant tail fibres you now cut off a few more and tie them in by their tips and, just as you tied in

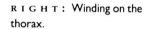

RIGHT: Winding on the thorax.

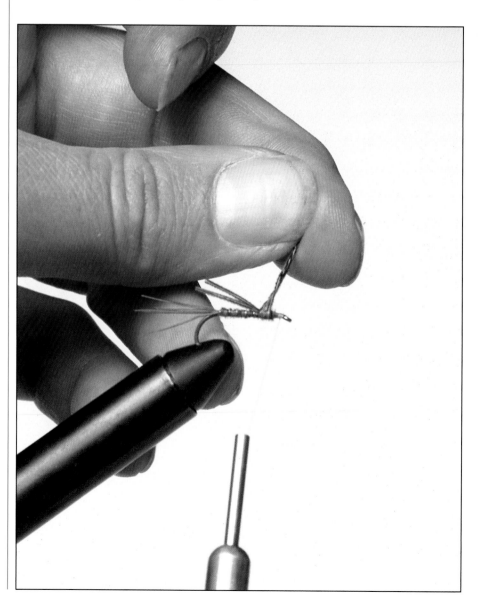

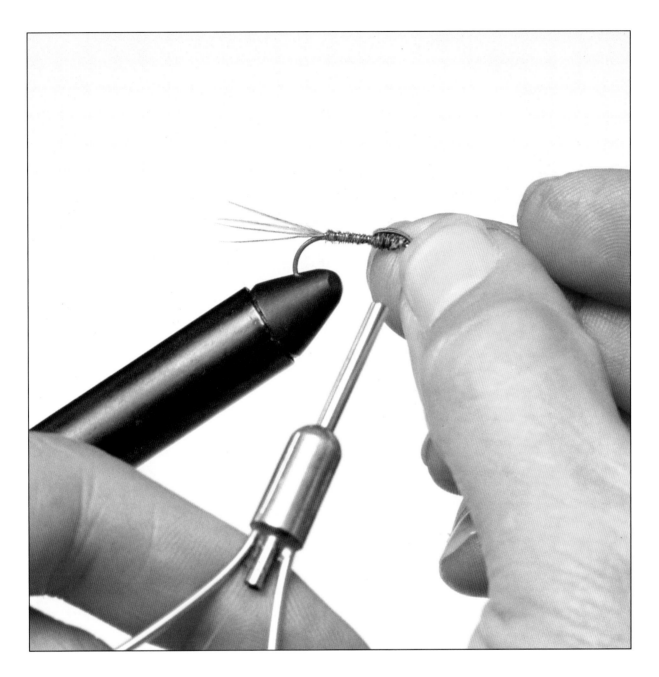

A B O V E : Fibres pulled over to make the wing cases.

the peacock herl in the very first fly, you lie them alongside the thread and wind the whole lot on so as to form a ball of a thorax. The thread which now twists in with the fibres strengthens them and prevents unravelling should a trout's teeth cut any of the fibres.

Tie off this twist of fibres just close to the hook eye and cut away the waste ends before bringing the remaining fibre ends over the top of the newly formed thorax to form the thorax case. Tie them down, cut off the excess and the fly is then ready for a whip finish and is complete, a pheasant tail nymph. There are endless variations on this pattern but this is the basis of them all.

D U B B I N G

I have left what is probably the most feared aspect of fly tying to the last if only because it merely follows on in a logical progression of techniques and once you have mastered this the last of my preliminary fly tying techniques you are ready to tackle virtually any fly.

Dubbing involves the application of individual fibres of hair to the tying thread which is then wound round the body or thorax of the fly to be tied and in so doing the hairs become trapped by the thread and stand out from the hook as a sort of fuzz. I taught myself how to dub and it was a long and painful process during which I tried all sorts of ways of getting those horrible bits of fur to stay attached to the thread, some more successful than others.

I tried using the liquid wax to make the thread more tacky, this was in the days before prewaxed threads, and succeeded in making everything else but the fur into a sticky mass. It was many years before I devised the technique I have used ever since and it came about when I first started commercially to tie flies for Taff Price. Speed was of the essence then and one day, when trying to be quick, I suddenly found that I could dub very easily indeed and have since demonstrated this method to club meetings and shows over many years and it has won many converts, especially among newcomers to fly tying.

I will first describe the technique and then we will use it to make a nymph.

Put a hook in the vice, a long-shank pattern, and attach the thread anywhere along the shank.

Take a pinch of the seal's fur substitute, any colour will do at this stage, and fold it up between your fingers so as to crush and bend the fibres. Squash it up until you can roll it in the palm of your hand and it will stay like a little ball, Now all the fibres are mangled and squashed and grip each other very well. Take hold of a piece of this ball and gradually tease the fibres out until you get what looks like a stretched-out web of material. It holds together very well, all the fibres gripping each other with their little bends and kinks.

RIGHT: Hair to be used for a dubbed body.

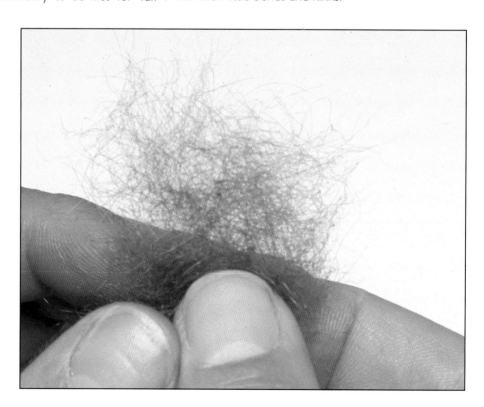

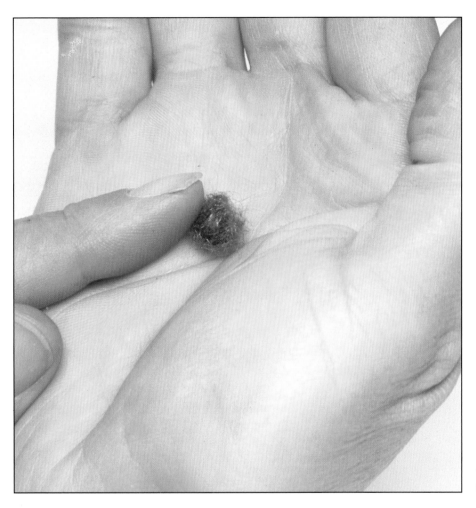

L E F T : The fibres folded
and rolled into a tight ball.

R I G H T : The ball teased
out to make a web of fibres.

RIGHT: The web of fibres on the thread and trapped by the left thumb.

BELOW: The web being twisted around the thread.

Lay this web of material on top of the tying thread with one end touching the hook shank and place your left thumb on the end so that it is trapped against the hook. You can now let go with the right hand and the fibre web will stay hanging from the hook.

Now twist the web of hairs round the tying thread in one direction only, clockwise, and it will very quickly form a rope with the thread.

Use the thumb and middle finger of your right hand, having first wetted each one with your tongue. Gently twist the web round the thread for two turns and then apply more pressure to twist it round the thread quite firmly. As you do so you must slowly move your fingers down the thread while all the time keeping the left thumb in position.

When the rope of material has formed you can thin it out by pulling the web of hair apart slightly and twisting again. When you are satisfied with the rope, i.e. it is nice and evenly spread with the hairs, you can now take one turn round the hook shank which will have the effect of trapping the end fibres formerly held by your left thumb and you are now free to wind the rope of hair round the hook to make the dubbed body.

It is quite easy to make the whole of a long-shank 8 body in one operation with this method and if, as you wind the rope along the shank it begins to loosen, it is a simple matter to tighten the twist. You can put on as much or as little as you like and the whole lot will cling together very well. The use of very short-fibred hair is not quite so easy with this technique and it is better to learn with hair which has a fibre length of ½- to one-in or more. From the materials in our basic selection it is possible to put together a very effective nymph using a dubbed body.

L E F T : **The rope effect of the twisted web.**

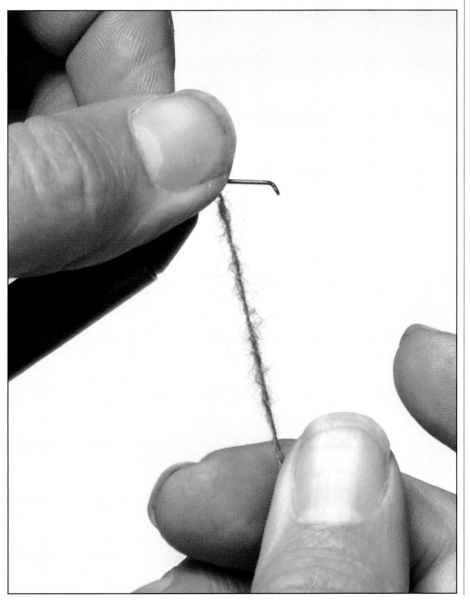

ABOVE: Take a turn around the hook to trap the ends previously held by the left thumb.

LEFT: The completed body, with the dubbing being picked out.

Start by tying in a tail of cock pheasant feather fibres, four or five will do, and then tie in a length of gold wire which will be the ribbing later on.

The body can now be made of dubbed green seal's fur substitute prepared exactly as I have just described, and with the rope wound so as to produce a taper to the body, i.e. thin at the tail and getting thicker up towards the eye. Take the dubbing about two-thirds of the way up the shank and finish it off before winding up the gold wire rib on the opposite spiral. On this kind of body you can see clearly how the ribbing would disappear into the body material if wound in the same direction.

Tie off the ribbing and then for the remaining third of the shank length dub on some of the brown seal's fur substitute and finally finish off with a brown hen hackle.

Once again emphasising that proportioning is all-important when making dubbed bodies and for a nymph the adage of two-thirds abdomen and one-third thorax will always hold true but you should try to achieve a neatly tapering body rather than a bulky one. If a pattern calls for the appearance of bulk then it is a simple matter to pick out the hairs with the dubbing needle, for that is its true purpose.

Although we are imitating or suggesting nymphs with our tyings it so happens time and time again that the best pattern proves to be the shaggiest-looking one which when compared with the natural creature bears no resemblance, but is this not what fly fishing is all about? It is the taking of a fish on a creation of fur and feather.

With dubbing mastered, the basics of fly tying are now complete and at this stage in a series of lessons I would usually ask my class to tie up a pattern combining most of the techniques may have learnt, just to show how well each one has progressed from the early fumblings with peacock herl and a black hen feather.

Bearing in mind the limitations of our initial material list, I think that a split-wing pheasant tail would be a good test, so here is the layout of the pattern and an example in the photograph.

Hook: Size 12 up-eye
Tail: Three fibres of cock pheasant (rooster) tail
Rib: Fine gold wire
Body: Three fibres of cock pheasant wound for two-thirds of the shank
Wings: Grey mallard tied upright and split
Hackle: Red game cock

FLY PATTERNS

Test Magnificence in the shape of a 5lb brown and a rainbow from the Mecca of fly fishers the world over, Hampshire's River Test.

This last section comprises a broad selection of flies from the four categories of patterns. The text lists suggested hook sizes and the component tying of the pattern, along with a brief description of best conditions for using each fly.

Changing from hen to cock hackles will convert the patterns to simple dry flies. An all black fly with a silver rib becomes a Williams Favourite. Change the tail to red wool and palmer up a cock hackle and you have a Zulu, a red wool body and tail with a palmered, red game, cock hackle becomes a Soldier Palmer. You will soon concoct your own variations on the basic theme and believe me – they will catch fish.

Returning a fly-caught Chinook to the Wind River in Washington.

STANDARD
WET FLIES

A B O V E : A fresh run grilse (Atlantic Salmon) from
the River Drowse in Ireland, caught on a Teeny Nymph.

~~~~~ LIGHT CAHILL ~~~~~

A long established American wet fly, equally effective in dry or nymph form; all tyings are included here because of its all round fish-taking ability.

Hook: 16-8 standard shank
Tail: cream hackle fibres
Body: cream seals fur sub
Hackle: ginger hen hackle tied false
Wing: wood duck fibres

~~~~~ ALEXANDRA ~~~~~~

This is a showy fly which imitates nothing and yet in true wet fly mould it is a remarkable fish catcher. Many times the colour combination of red, black and silver will occur in fly patterns.

Hook: 6-12 standard shank
Tail: red feather fibres
Body: flat silver tinsel
Hackle: black hen tied false
Wing: peacock sword feathers with slips of red feather alongside

~~~~~~ HORNBERG ~~~~~~~~

I don't think that this fly knows quite whether to be a dry, wet, or lure, but fished as a wet fly it works well and is so different that the fish maybe take it out of curiosity.

Hook: 12-8 standard shank
Body: flat silver tinsel
Wing: silver mallard feather with the tips varnished to bring them together and with cheeks of jungle cock or substitute
Hackle: ginger or cree cock hackle wound full

~~ PARMACHENE BELLE ~~

An attractor wet fly that is pleasing to look at, demanding to tie and deadly when fished in bright sun and clear water. Use a long leader and fish it very slowly just under the surface.

Hook: 12-8 standard shank
Tail: red and white cock hackle fibres
Body: yellow floss with flat gold rib
Hackle: red and white cock fibres tied false
Wing: married strips of red and white goose

~~~ WICKHAM'S FANCY ~~~

A pattern that fishes well when caddis flies are on the move or as a general attractor all year round and the basis of the early stages in this book.

Hooks: 16-8 standard shank
Tail: red game cock hackle fibres
Body: gold tinsel with wire rib
Hackle: palmered red game cock
Wing: grey mallard

~~~~~~~~ INVICTA ~~~~~~~~

Another famous pattern for when the adult caddis/sedge are on the move, particularly in the evenings. Not an easy pattern to tie well; an excellent test of skills.

Hooks: 14-8 standard shank
Tail: golden pheasant crest
Body: dubbed yellow/amber seals fur sub with a palmered red game cock hackle and an oval gold rib
Hackle: blue jay tied false
Wing: hen pheasant centre tail

~ TEAL BLUE AND SILVER ~

Not many patterns use blue but it is very attractive to fresh migratory fish and this fly is a special for sea trout, the migratory form of browns.

Hooks: 14-8 standard shank
Tail: golden pheasant tippets
Body: silver tinsel with wire rib
Hackle: blue hen tied false
Wing: teal flank feathers

~~~~~~ PETER ROSS ~~~~~~

Just look at the colour combination again but this time combined with the striped effect, which is another trigger to a predatory fish mind.

Hooks: 16-8 standard shank
Tail: golden pheasant tippets
Body: 2/3 silver tinsel, 1/3 red wool or seals fur sub, all ribbed with silver wire
Hackle: black hen tied false
Wing: teal flank feather

~ MALLARD AND CLARET ~

Particularly good early in the season on river or lake and when chironomids are hatching.

Hooks: 16-8 standard shank
Tail: golden pheasant tippets
Body: claret seals fur sub or wool with gold rib
Hackle: claret or black hen
Wing: bronze mallard

~~~~~~~~~ ZULU ~~~~~~~~~

The black, red, and silver combination again. A great favourite in waters that are poor food producers and where the fish have to be opportunist feeders.

Hooks: 16-8 standard shank
Tail: red wool
Body: black wool or seals fur sub
Hackle: black cock, sometimes palmered

~~~~~~~~~ BIBIO ~~~~~~~~~

Just how many permutations are possible. Here is another deadly pattern using the primary trout colours.

Hooks: 12-8 standard shank
Body: black seals fur sub or wool with small red section in the middle
Hackle: black cock palmered with a silver wire rib

~~~~ SOLDIER PALMER ~~~~

A marvellous fly for the top dropper position on a wet fly cast as if fished in the surface film it resembles an insect struggling to emerge.

Hooks: 16-8 standard shank
Body: dubbed red seals fur substitute
Hackle: red game cock palmered with gold wire rib

~~~ WATSON'S FANCY ~~~

Yet another in the black/red/silver mould and a real test of a fly tier's skills. I once had to make 12 dozen of this one in size 16 for an order; what a job that was.

Hook: 14-8 standard shank
Tail: golden pheasant crest
Body: half black, half red wool with silver rib
Hackle: black hen tied false
Wing: slips of black crow with cheeks of jungle cock

~ WOODCOCK AND GREEN ~

A tried and tested pattern that is very good when fished in the upper layers during a hatch from stillwater.

Hook: 16-8 standard shank
Tail: golden pheasant tippets
Body: green seals fur sub ribbed with gold tinsel
Hackle: pale green tied false
Wing: woodcock wing quills

~~~~~ KINGSMILL ~~~~~~ GREEN BUTT

A fluo green butt in association with a black-based fly makes a deadly combination and in this standard wet-fly form, you have in effect a mini modern lure.

Hook: 14-10 standard shank
Tail: golden pheasant crest
Body: fluo green floss butt followed by silver ribbed black ostrich herl
Hackle: black hen tied false
Wing: black crow with jungle cock cheeks and golden pheasant crest topping

~~~~ BLACK PENNELL ~~~~

One of the best flies I know when chironomids are hatching on lakes; in larger sizes it takes sea trout and tied bushy is a great dapping fly.

Hook: 14-8 standard shank
Tail: golden pheasant tippets
Body: butt of silver wire then ribbed over black floss
Hackle: black cock tied long in the fibre

~ CINNAMON AND GOLD ~

This lovely old pattern is not only a good fish catcher it's also good to look at and satisfying to tie.

Hook: 12-8 standard shank
Tail: golden pheasant tippets
Body: flat gold tinsel
Hackle: ginger cock hackle fibres tied false
Wing: cinnamon hen wing quills

~ WILLIAM'S FAVOURITE ~

If times are hard on your favourite fishery or you are on a new water then use this pattern, it's back to basics with black and silver and it works time after time.

Hook: 16-10 standard shank
Tail: black hackle fibres
Body: black floss ribbed with silver wire
Hackle: black hen

~~~~~~~ DUNKELD ~~~~~~~

Tied in larger sizes and even up to salmon size this is a great fly for a bit of flash and glitter, especially good on sunny days worked through the top layers of water.

Hooks: 16-8 standard shank
Tail: golden pheasant crest
Body: gold tinsel with wire rib
Hackle: hot orange cock tied false
Wing: bronze mallard

~~~~~~~ BUTCHER ~~~~~~~

Once again the combination of black, red and silver, this is not an easy pattern to tie well because of the difficult wing material, but it is an excellent fish catcher.

Hooks: 16-8 standard shank
Tail: red ibis substitute
Body: silver tinsel with wire rib
Hackle: black hen tied false
Wing: blue mallard

~~~~ SILVER INVICTA ~~~~

A look at the best flies on fishery reports will see this pattern come to prominence in July when the coarse fish are around and it is an excellent imitation of a pin fry as well as being a good all round pattern.

Hook: 14-8 standard shank
Tail: golden pheasant crest
Body: silver tinsel with palmered red game cock hackle and wire rib
Hackle: blue jay fibres tied false
Wings: hen pheasant centre tail feathers

~~~~~ HENDRICKSON ~~~~~

Although conceived as a nymph this fly has adapted well to tying as a wet and is now a classic North American pattern for freestone waters.

Hook: 12-8 standard shank
Tail: wood duck flank fibres
Body: dark grey/brown for dubbing with brown thread rib
Hackle: brown partridge
Wing: wood duck flank fibres

~~~ GREENWELLS GLORY ~~~

This fly has been around a long time and caught many trout for anglers all over the world and I am quite sure will continue to do so as long as there are trout to be caught.

Hook: 14-8 standard shank
Tail: greenwell hen hackle fibres (ginger with black centre and sometimes omitted)
Body: yellow tying thread darkened with wax and ribbed with golden wire
Hackle: hen greenwell tied false
Wing: starling dyed brownish green

L U R E S

Timeless elegance, a river
keeper's hut on the River
Kennet, England.

~~~~~ JERSEY HERD ~~~~~

An English reservoir pattern attributed to Tom Ivens. An excellent all-round fly, but at its best around fry time at the back end of the year.

Hook: 6-20 longshank
Tail, back and head: peacock herl
Body: copper coloured tinsel
Hackle: hot orange cock wound full

~~~~~ LIGHT SPRUCE ~~~~~

A commonly used streamer pattern for trout on the West coast of America but almost unknown in the UK.

Hook: 6-10 longshank
Tail: peacock sword feather
Body: red floss and peacock herl
Hackle: badger cock wound full
Wing: badger cock hackles tied streamer style

~~~~ SILVER DARTER ~~~~

An American favourite that has found success all over the world and is especially good in broken water.

Hook: 6-10 longshank
Tail: silver mylar tubing
Hackle: peacock sword feather

~~~ MUDDLER MINNOW ~~~

Originally created by Don Gapen in the USA to imitate a small minnow in the streams, and now in a wide variety of options. Effective bumbled over the bottom or stripped over the surface.

Hook: 6-10 longshank
Tail: oak turkey (use hen pheasant centre tail as a sub)
Body: flat gold tinsel with wire rib
Wing: grey squirrel sheathed with oak turkey
Head: deer hair flared and clipped

~~ BLACK AND ORANGE ~~
MARABOU

One of Taff Price's inventions that has taken a great many fish by exploiting the amazing mobility of marabou.

Hook: 6-10 longshank
Tail: orange cock hackle fibres
Body: flat gold tinsel with oval rib
Hackle: orange cock hackle fibres
Wing: black marabou sometimes with jungle cock cheeks

~~~~~ MRS SIMPSON ~~~~~

An unusual style of fly of which there are a number of varieties all of which involved feathers tied in along the sides of the hook. Gives a very dense silhouette to the fly.

Hook: 6-10 longshank
Tail: black squirrel tail
Body: red floss
Hackle: three pairs of cock pheasant body feathers tied in at intervals along the shank

~~~~ YELLOW MATUKA ~~~~

A New Zealand pattern which catches well anywhere but especially where trout feed on bait fish in lakes.

Hook: 6-10 longshank
Tail and wing: well marked hen greenwell feathers
Body: yellow floss ribbed with oval gold
Hackle: hen greenwell

~~~~ WOOLLY BUGGER ~~~~

Very simple pattern and yet quite deadly, especially in cold water when fished low and deep. Must be the easiest to tie.

Hook: 10-6 longshank
Tail: black hackle fibres
Body: black chenille with palmered black hackle

~~~~ BLACK MARABOU ~~~~ MUDDLER

Yet another muddler variant and, surprise, surprise, here is the red, black and silver combination again.

Hook: 6-10 longshank
Tail: red feather fibres
Body: flat silver tinsel with wire rib
Wing: black marabou fibres
Head: deer hair flared and clipped

~~~~ ACE OF SPADES ~~~~

Essentially a black lure variant but tied matuka style with an overwing so as to give a solid profile and prevent the wing tangling under the hook bend.

Hook: 6-10 longshank
Tail and back: hen hackles dyed black
Rib: oval silver tinsel
Hackle: guinea fowl tied false
Over wing: bronze mallard

~~~~ DAVES SCULPIN ~~~~

A muddler variation which works well when fished slow and deep, particularly for older, well established fish that have turned completely predatory.

Hook: 10-4 longshank
Body: creamy yellow wool
Wing: matuka style cree cock
Rib: oval gold
Over wing: brown squirrel fibres
Fins: hen pheasant body feathers
Head: bands of coloured deer hair tied muddler style

~~~~ DOG NOBBLER ~~~~

This is a modern variation of an early type of jig fly and which is very effective on newly stocked trout. The undulating action of the tail induced by the lead head makes the fly swim enticingly.

Hook: 6-10 standard or longshank with a split shot crimped and glued to the head
Tail: bunch of marabou fibres, any colour and related to rest of fly
Body: chenille with palmered cock hackle and tinsel over rib
Head: eye effect painted on the shot

~~~~~~~ WHISKY ~~~~~~~
Orange is a wonderful colour for rainbow trout, especially in the summer months. It can provoke the fish into quite literally attacking the fly. The whisky fly is a great lure and a simple pattern to tie.
Hook: 6-12 longshank
Tail: hot orange cock hackle fibres
Body: gold tinsel with rib of flou orange floss
Hackle: hot orange cock tied false
Wing: orange calf or squirrel tail

~~~~~ BLACK GHOST ~~~~~
Wherever fish feed on fry the black ghost will catch them. It is a truly excellent pattern from the US.
Hook: 6-10 longshank
Tail: yellow hackle fibres or golden pheasant crest
Body: black floss ribbed with silver oval or flat
False hackle: yellow cock hackle fibres
Wing: four white cock hackle fibres tied streamer-style

~~~~~ MICKY FINN ~~~~~
This is a great pattern for the aggressive rainbow when the water warms up and they will chase a fly; but it also works well for many other species, specially when the water is coloured.
Hook: 6-10 longshank
Body: Flat silver ribbed with oval silver
Wing: in three parts, yellow, red and yellow bucktail, squirrel for the smaller sizes

~~~~~ SWEENY TODD ~~~~~
A Richard Walker invention using the time-honoured colour combination of red, black and silver to make a modern and highly effective lure.
Hook: 6-20 longshank
Body: black floss with oval silver rib
Collar: neon magenta floss
Hackle: red cock fibres tied false
Wing: black squirrel tail

~~~~~ MUNRO KILLER ~~~~~

A hair wing version of modern salmon flies that is easy to make and every bit as effective as complicated feather wing patterns.

Hook: 4-12 up eye salmon iron
Tag: oval gold
Body: black floss with oval gold rib
Hackle: hot orange cock and dyed blue guinea fowl
Wing: yellow bucktail with black over, squirrel for smaller flies

~~~~~~ BLUE CHARM ~~~~~~

This is a recognised salmon fly but in reality is just a lure and shows how salmon flies can be simply tied with feather wings. Actually quite difficult to get well proportioned.

Hook: 4-12 up eye salmon
Tag: oval silver
Tail: golden pheasant crest and black ostrich as a butt
Body: black floss with oval silver rib
Hackle: blue cock
Wing: bronze mallard with teal over wing and golden pheasant crest as a topping

~~~~~ POLYSTICKLE ~~~~~

Another Richard Walker pattern which is intended to imitate a small fish and show its translucence. It comes under the general heading of lures and as you can see uses very little natural material in its tying.

Hook: 6-12 longshank
Tail and back: raffene
Body: black floss rib over silver then red floss and all over wound with strip of clear polythene
Hackle: red or orange cock hackle tied false

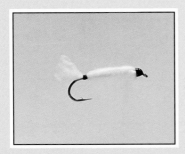

~~~~~~ A P P E T I Z E R ~~~~~~
A white based English pattern which is an excellent lure for fry feeders and makes use of the mobility of marabou for its enticing action.
Hook: 6-10 longshank
Tail: mixed fibres of silver mallard, orange and green cock hackle fibres
Body: white chenille ribbed with silver oval
Hackle: same mix as tail and tied false
Wing: white marabou with grey squirrel over

~~~~~~ B A B Y D O L L ~~~~~~
So called because it was apparently first tied using the white wool from baby's clothes, this pattern is tied in a fish shape, but it relies on the glow of the white wool to attract fish. White has always been a good lure colour, especially at fry time.
Hook: 6-10 long or standard shank
Tail, body, back: all of white 'baby' wool

~~~ R O Y A L C O A C H M A N ~~~
B U C K T A I L
A North American variation on an old pattern which has turned an already good fly into an excellent lure.
Hook: 6-10 longshank
Tail: golden pheasant tippetts
Body: red floss with ends of peacock herl
Hackle: brown cock tied false
Wing: white bucktail fibres

~~~~~ PEARL ZONKER ~~~~~

The technique of using strips of fur tied in Matuka style is very popular nowadays; the pearl mylar tubing makes a great fish scale effect.

Hook: 4-10 longshank
Body: pearl mylar tubing
Wing: thin strip of white rabbit tied matuka style at either end of the body
Hackle: red cock wound full

~~~~ CAT'S WHISKER ~~~~

Another white-based fly for fry feeders and mated with fluo yellow chenille to deadly effect.

Hook: 6-10 longshank
Tail: tuft of white marabou
Body: fluo yellow chenille
Wing: tuft of white marabou
Head: pair of bead chain eyes

~~~~~ GIRDLE BUG ~~~~~~

Born from a type of Bass fly, this is an American pattern through and through. Quite what it represents I doubt that anyone knows but fish take it well. I once had an Irish salmon on one.

Hook: 4-12 longshank
Tail and legs: white or black living rubber
Body: chenille in a range of colours

≈ 99 ≈

NYMPHS

Fresh from the sea, a 25-inch
Char caught in Alaska.

~~~~~~ P V C N Y M P H ~~~~~~

A John Goddard pattern, the abdomen is covered with stretched PVC to give the nymph a lifelike appearance. Very good on rivers when a hatch is on.

Hook: 12-16 standard shank
Tail: olive dyed feather fibre
Abdomen: olive feather with stretched PVC over
Thorax: olive feather fibre with brownish feather fibre wing case

~~~~~ B L A C K N Y M P H ~~~~~

One of the most basic tyings you can do for a nymph and absolutely invaluable to have in the box. Black works anywhere in the world for the fly fisher.

Hook: 8-14 standard shank
Tail: black hackle fibres
Body: black seals fur sub ribbed with silver wire
Thorax: black seals fur sub with grey feather fibre over

~~~~ D A M S E L N Y M P H ~~~~

It's stretching credulity to call this fly an imitation of the damsel nymph but it's a fact that trout feeding on the natural will take this pattern very well indeed.

Hook: 8-12 longshank
Tail: green hackle fibres
Body: seals fur substitute, multi-colour mix
Rib: gold oval
Hackle: golden olive dyed partridge

~~~~~~~ Z U G B U G ~~~~~~~

A generalized nymph pattern that originated in America and has since proved its worth in all waters that hold trout. It can be very good when fished weighted.

Hook: 10-14 standard shank
Tail: peacock sword
Body: peacock herl, ribbed flat silver
Hackle: brown hen
Wing: wood duck

~~~~ SWANNUNDAZE ~~~~
STONEFLY

An excellent pattern that makes full use of the translucence obtained by the use of swannundaze, a plastic which is flat one side and oval on the other.

Hook: 6-8 longshank, bent to suggest the humped pupa

Tail: brown goose biots

Abdomen: mixed golden yellow and grey seals fur sub dubbed heavily and ribbed with amber swannundaze

Thorax: similar dubbing mix with the wing cases being formed by laying a brown speckled partridge feather along the back and overlaying a striped partridge feather

~~~~~~~~ PRINCE ~~~~~~~~

An interesting fly in that it looks 'buggy' and yet actually resembles nothing specific. The white feather slips seem to act as an attractant to the fish.

Hook: 8-12 standard shank

Tail: brown goose biot

Body: peacock herl with flat gold rib

Hackle: brown hen

Horns: slips of white goose or swan

~~~ MONTANA NYMPH ~~~

A dressing of the Stone Fly Larva initiated in Montana and now used worldwide. A general-purpose pattern where the Stone Fly does not occur and in Europe it is little other than a variant of the black lure.

Hook: 12-8 longshank, often weighted

Tail: black cock hackle tips or bunch of black cock hackle fibres

Abdomen: black chenille

Thorax: yellow chenille with variants using fluo green, white or orange

Wing case: black chenille

Hackle: Black cock wound through the thorax

~~~~~ GOLD RIBBED ~~~~~
HARE'S EAR

This is a fly that catches any trout that is feeding on ephemerid (mayfly) nymphs, and also works as a general nymph pattern right throughout the year.

Hook: 8-16 standard shank

Tail: ginger hackle fibres or longer hairs from a hare's mask

Body: dubbed hare's ear ribbed with gold tinsel

Thorax: dubbed hare's ear picked out with feather fibre wing case

~~ AMERICAN MARABOU ~~ DAMSEL

This tying has become amazingly successful in the UK in recent years. It really comes into its own when the damsel larvae are active during the main part of the day.

Hook: 8-12 longshank

Tail: tuft of olive marabou fibres

Abdomen: twisted olive marabou

Thorax: dubbed olive seals fur sub with short-fibred olive hackle half way through and wing cases of olive feather fibre

Head: bright green beads

~~~~~ SAWYER'S PTN ~~~~~

A classic the world over and a remarkably effective nymph dressing. Invented by Frank Sawyer, the river keeper from Hampshire, England. Unusual in that the tying thread is replaced by fine copper wire which acts as the pattern's weight.

Hook: 10-18 standard shank

Tail, body and thorax: pheasant tail (rooster) fibres

~ MEDIUM ALL PURPOSE ~ NYMPH

This pattern is the American equivalent of the English angler's GRHE, it typifies the greater variety of detail of American flies in that it comes in three shades.

Hook: 8-12 longshank

Tail: pheasant tail fibres

Body: grey brown polydubbing ribbed with clear nylon

Wing case: grouse hackle with the ends bent back to form the legs

~~~~~ EARLY BROWN ~~~~~ STONEFLY

An ideal pattern for the streams where the stonefly features strongly in the fish diet.

Hook: 8-10 longshank

Tail: brown hen hackle fibres

Abdomen: dubbed grey rabbit underfur with a pale plastic rib

Thorax: grey rabbit underfur mixed with guard hairs well picked out and with wing cases of pale brown feather fibre

~~~~~ C A S E D   C A D D I S ~~~~~

Larvae of the stonefly (caddis) make up the greater part of a trout's diet, especially in the early season, and imitations of the larval form fished along the bottom are very successful.

Hook: 8-12 longshank
Body: blue underfur from a rabbit dubbed onto silver tinsel chenille and wound
Head: black ostrich herl

~~~~~ T E E N Y   N Y M P H ~~~~~

Invented by Oregon's steelhead king, Jim Teeny, this fly was to be a broad band pattern suitable for all species and simple to tie so there would be no fear of fishing it in snaggy places. Tied in a variety of colours and only using rooster (cock pheasant) tail fibres.

Hook: 12 short shank to 2 longshank
Body, false hackles: tail feather fibres from a rooster (cock pheasant) sometimes tied with a wing of the same material on the larger hooks

~~~~~ G R E E N   B I T C H ~~~~~
CREEK NYMPH

A modern American tying using living rubber for its action; a general stone fly pattern.

Hook: 6-10 longshank
Tail: two pieces of living rubber
Body: woven from fluo green and black chenille
Thorax: black chenille with red game cock hackle palmered through it
Head: two more pieces of living rubber

~ C O C K W I L L S   R E D   B R O W N ~

Based on a reservoir pattern by the late Tom Ivens and intended to represent the coloration of the male stickleback at breeding time, this fly has proved to be a very good general-purpose nymph for most stillwaters.

Hook: 10 longshank
Tail, back and head: four fibres of peacock herl
Body: copper golfingering ribbed with a strand of brown ostrich herl and copper wire
Thorax: two turns of neon magenta chenille

~~ GREEN THORAX PTN ~~

A variant on the pheasant tail series and using green fluo which attracts trout so well. Used as a general purpose nymph or fished fast at fry time.

Hook: 8-12 longshank
Tail: pheasant tail fibres
Body: pheasant tail fibres ribbed with copper wire
Thorax: fluo green floss with pheasant fibres over
Hackle: ginger cock tied false

~~ COLONEL'S CREEPER ~~

An all-purpose nymph that would make an excellent stonefly imitation and has found great success in English stillwaters.

Hook: 8-10 longshank
Tail: bunch of olive dyed rabbit fur
Body: weighted along the sides of the hook to widen it then dubbed olive seals fur sub ribbed with nylon
Thorax: dressed upside down and made with two wing cases of varnished raffene and legs of olive goose biots in among the dubbed olive seals fur sub

~~~~~~~ LEAD BUG ~~~~~~~

One of the author's patterns and designed for use on large fish which can be targetted in clear water. It gives a very approximate suggestion of a nymph, with its segmented body and thorax hump, and is intended to sink very rapidly, yet not be too heavy.

Hook: 10 to 12 standard shank
Tail: olive floss
Abdomen: fine lead wire
Thorax, wing case and leg stubs: olive floss

~~~~ G O L D E N   S H R I M P ~~~~

The shrimp is a drab greenish or brown hue, although when changing its skin it is very much paler; many anglers feel that the golden shrimp somehow appears to be vulnerable to the trout. Whatever the truth, the fly is very successful.

Hook: 10 or 12 standard shank, a Sedge pattern is very good
Tail: fibres of golden olive cock hackle
Body: golden olive seals fur or substitute
Hackle: palmered golden olive cock
Back: yellow dyed latex
Rib: gold wire

~~~~~ L I G H T   C A H I L L ~~~~~

A truly excellent general-purpose nymph for all epheremid/mayfly patterns in streams. North American in origin and no fly box should be without it.

Hook: 10-18 standard shank
Tail: wood duck fibres
Body: creamy seals fur substitute
Hackle: ginger hen fibres
Wing case: wood duck

~~~~ G R E E N   C H O M P E R ~~~~

A remarkably easy pattern to tie and it can suggest all manner of aquatic life. The fish certainly think it looks edible and the colour can be varied according to water and season.

Hook: 10-14 standard shank
Back: raffene
Body: ostrich herl

DRY FLIES

Tranquility in the setting of a
small lake at Wintershall in
Surrey.

~~~~~ ROYAL WULFF ~~~~~

One of Lee Wulff's all time greats and a wonderful general purpose dry that rides rough water very well and is taken by all species.

Hook: 8-12 standard shank
Tail: black squirrel hair
Body: red floss with peacock herl either end
Wings: white calf tail
Hackle: two red game cock hackles

~~~ CINNAMON SEDGE ~~~

A very effective broad band sedge pattern, not just for when the actual cinnamon sedge is hatching. Equally effective on rivers or lakes.

Hook: 10-14 up eye
Body: cinnamon feather fibre with palmered ginger cock hackle and gold wire rib
Wings: cinnamon hen quills
Hackle: ginger cock hackle

~~ FRENCH PARTRIDGE ~~ MAYFLY

An all-time English favourite for the annual mayfly carnival when the trout gorge themselves on this large insect. There may be more efficient patterns, but this one is so pretty.

Hook: special mayfly 8-10 longshank
Tail: cock pheasant fibres
Body: natural raffia ribbed with red thread and an olive cock hackle and gold wire
Hackle: French partridge flank feather

~~~ DADDY LONG LEGS ~~~ (CRANE FLY)

A large terrestrial that trout love to eat and which in late summer can hatch in enormous numbers.

Hook: 8-12 longshank
Body: detached end of closely bunched dyed deer hair
Legs: knotted cock pheasant tail fibres
Wings: cree hackle points
Hackle: two ginger cock hackles wound full

~~~ ELK HAIR HOPPER ~~~

Hoppers are a great fly to fish in the summer in the USA when they are cast at the edges of the stream. Now they are being used in Europe but more as general purpose dries on lakes.

Hook: 8-12 longshank
Tail: red dyed squirrel hair
Body: yellow floss ribbed with clipped Grizzle hackle
Wing: bunch of elk hair
Hackle: two cree cock hackles

~~~~~ LIGHT CAHILL ~~~~~

Thought to be at least a hundred years old, this pattern is very effective when the paler ephemerids are hatching, especially in the evening when it is easy to see.

Hook: 12-16 standard shank
Tail: cream hackle fibres
Body: cream seals fur substitute
Wings: wood duck
Hackle: cream cock hackle

~~~~ YELLOW HUMPY ~~~~

A wonderful floater for rough water, originally from the freestone rivers of Western America.

Hook: 10-14 standard shank
Tail: moose fibres
Body: yellow floss with the moose fibres tied over the top
Wing: ends of a bunch of moose fibres
Hackle: two grizzle cock hackles

~ STRADDLEBUG MAYFLY ~

Interesting variation for mayfly in that this pattern has an orange hackle which makes it stand out from all the others. It often gets taken when the fish are full to the gills with the natural.

Hook: 8-12 longshank
Tail: cock pheasant fibres
Body: natural raffia ribbed with gold wire
Hackle: two wound together, hot orange cock and summer duck feather
Head: peacock herl

~RICHARD WALKER SEDGE~

The ever inventive Richard Walker produced this pattern to have a sedge (caddis) profile; the long hackle was so that the fly could be stripped back over the surface to imitate the adults skittering motion.

Hook: 8-12 standard shank
Butt: hot orange floss
Body: cock pheasant fibres
Wing: red game cock hackle fibres
Hackle: red game cock hackle, long fibred

~~~~ BLACK BIVISIBLE ~~~~

A fly that relies on merely suggesting an adult insect by its straggly hackle and fuzzy outline. It has the advantage of riding very well and being easy for the angler to see and tie.

Hook: 10-14 standard shank
Tail: black cock hackle fibres
Body: palmered black cock hackle
Hackle: white cock hackle

~~ DARK HENDRICKSON ~~

A famous standard American dry that catches well when the mayfly species hatch and scores on most waters as a general pattern.

Hook: 12-18 standard shank
Tail: dark dun or grey cock hackle fibres
Body: dubbed muskrat under fur
Wing: wood duck
Hackle: dark dun or grey cock hackle

~~~~~ BLACK GNAT ~~~~~~

A black dry fly is essential at times, especially in early season when the natural hatches.

Hook: 10-18 up eye
Tail: black cock hackle fibres
Body: black floss
Wings: grey mallard or starling
Hackle: black cock wound full

~~~~ QUILL GORDON ~~~~
A pattern from the Catskills in New York State,
often used in the UK as an alternative to standard
olive patterns when the natural is hatching.

Hook: 12-18 standard shank
Tail: light brown or grey cock hackle fibres
Body: stripped peacock quill
Wings: wood duck
Hackle: medium dun cock or grey cock

~~ BLUE WINGED OLIVE ~~
This imitation of a commonly occurring fly is a
standard for when the fly hatches and is essential for
anyone who fishes limestone (chalk) waters.

Hook: 14-16 standard shank
Tail: dark dun hackle fibres, grey will suffice
Body: dubbed olive grey fur
Wings: blue dun hackle tips
Hackle: dark dun cock or grey hackle

~~~~~~~ ADAMS ~~~~~~~~
This American fly is now much used on English chalk
streams, especially when olives are hatching. It also
makes a good lake dry fly.

Hook: 10-20 standard shank
Tail: mixed brown and grizzle cock hackle fibres
Body: muskrat under fur dubbed
Wing: grizzle hackle tips
Hackle: mixed red game and grizzle

~~~ WICKHAMS FANCY ~~~
A flashy dry fly that serves well when there is a
sedge hatch or when the water is rough and the sun
bright when its wink of gold brings the fish up.

Hook: 16-8 standard shank
Tail: red game cock hackle fibres
Body: gold tinsel with palmered red game cock hackle
and gold wire rib
Wings: grey mallard or starling
Hackle: red game cock hackle

~BLUE PHEASANT TAIL~

A fly of the rough water rivers which are fished best early in the year and will produce fish even when there is no hatch taking place.

Hook: 14-10 standard shank
Tail: pheasant tail fibres
Body: pheasant tail fibres with gold wire rib
Hackle: blue dun cock

~~~~~GREY DUSTER~~~~~

This is a wonderful pattern when all sorts of tiny smuts are on the water and trout are being 'difficult'. It will often fool the most crafty fish and yet is simplicity itself.

Hook: 18-12 standard shank
Body: dubbed rabbit under fur 'blueish grey'
Hackle: badger cock hackle 'white with black centre and tips'

~~LUNNS PARTICULAR~~

A classic Test fly and best when olive spinners are on the water but it serves for any fall of spent fly.

Hook: 16-14 up eye
Tail: fibres of red game cock hackle
Body: stripped red game cock hackle stem
Wings: blue dun hackle points tied spent
Hackle: red game cock hackle

OLIVE ELK
~~~~~WING CADDIS~~~~~

Quite an easy pattern to tie and the elk hair splay serves well to suggest the sedge (caddis) profile as well as making the fly float well.

Hook: 14-10 standard shank
Body: dubbed yellowish for substitute
Hackle: palmered red game cock hackle
Wing: elk hair with the butts lifted to make a head

ADDITIONAL MATERIALS IN COMMON USAGE

Hackles from either cock or hen come in a wide variety of natural colours as well as the myriad of dyed ones available and a good fly tying collection should include:

Grizzle, white, badger, honey and cree cock necks

White, ginger and greenwell hen

Dyed cock and hen in shades of olive, red, claret, orange, blue, green and yellow

Natural and dyed black, yellow and bleached white deer hair

Marabou plumes (in fact from the domestic turkey) in a wide range of dyed colours

Ostrich herl in a range of colours

Partridge feathers, English and French

A hare's mask, i.e. the complete face of the hare for a range of excellent dubbing material

BELOW: A wide selection of feathers which will enable many patterns to be tied.

Other tinsels such as oval silver and gold and copper wire

Golden pheasant crest and neck feathers

Dyed hairs in various colours, squirrel, bucktail and goat

Condor substitute, large quill feathers dyed in various colours

Man-made materials such as chenille, raffene, latex, swannudaze, flashabou, polythene and a wide range of other items used by fly tyers

Wing quills from starling, grouse, woodcock and speckled hen

Flank feathers from teal and wood duck

Bronze mallard feathers and, from the same bird, the blue wing coverts

A whole range of dubbing materials, some natural some man-made and in a wide variety of colours

This list may seem an intimidating one but once you are dedicated to fly tying you will inevitably accumulate most of the items on this list and a good many more!

Fly tying is all about inventiveness and you will try all manner of materials in an attempt to find that deadly, sure-fire, never-failing pattern.

ADDITIONAL TOOLS

At the beginning of this book I suggested that you acquire two pairs of scissors, one for feather and one for tinsel and so on. Now that you are well into fly tying I suggest that you buy a really first-class pair and just keep them for your better work with small flies.

A dubbing twister is a very useful gadget for tying dubbed bodies with short-fibres furs such as mole or hare's ear. It will more than earn its keep.

A hair stacker is a tube into which you slip long hairs which are to form wings and so on, and then by tapping the tube you can ensure that all the ends of the hairs are lined up.

A gallows tool enables parachute hackles to be tied with relative ease and it is a worth-while addition to your equipment.

Being an inventive lot, fly tyers are forever bringing out 'new' gadgets but you will rarely find professional tyers using any others than those tools I have listed. If a pro does not use a tool, be sure that it is not worth buying.

L E F T : A dubbing twister.

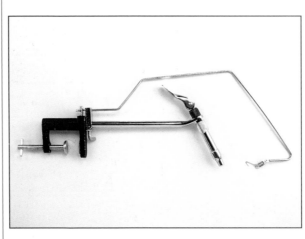

A B O V E : The Gallows tool for parachute hackles.

SPECIAL TECHNIQUES

Some of the additional materials I listed require that you learn a new method of tying in addition to the basic ones we mastered, and I will describe them now that you are able to move on to more adventurous fly tying.

DEER HAIR

This is a fun-material to use although in latter years it has been a nuisance to me as I have become allergic to it and have to take anti-histamine tablets before handling it. Deer hair is used mostly in forming the heads of Muddler patterns but has all kinds of other uses.

A single deer hair is a hollow tube and if, for example, you had a length of half an in copper pipe on a table and sharply compressed it at one point it would fold in half

LEFT : A bunch of deer hair ready for the muddler head.

and this also happens to deer hair when given the same treatment. We take a bunch of these hollow-tube hairs and compress them all at the same point so that the result is a flare of deer hair. Looked at in that context tying deer hair is no great problem. It is easiest first to tie deer hair on to a hook which only has a covering of tying thread to get the hang of the method.

Cut off a bunch of hair about as thick as a pencil, with the pointed ends projecting to your left. Offer the bunch up to the hook and lay it parallel with the shank before taking a loose turn of thread round it. Do not compress the fibre at this stage.

Make a second loose turn of thread in exactly the same place as the first and then pull slowly downwards with the bobbin and at the same time relax your hold on the bunch of hair. As the two loose turns of thread begin to tighten the bunch of hair will be compressed and start to flare out and at the same time turn round the hook shank so that by the time you have fully tightened the thread the hair will have flared all round the hook.

ABOVE: Two loose turns of thread around the bunch of hair.

RIGHT: Tightening the thread causes the hair to flare.

If making up a full head, you would form the thumb and two-finger pinch with the left hand and sweep the fibres back towards the hook bend and place a further bunch of hair on top of the hook shank. Repeat the operation to flare the hair and gradually build up a full head. It will now look like some kind of hairy monster and must be clipped to shape with scissors. You can make up your own shapes but in the photograph you will see that I have cut it to a conventional Muddler head and you can also see the reason for tying in the pointed ends of the hair off to the left. If you leave them uncut they form a rather neat collar hackle effect.

Now tie up a single Muddler using black wool for the body ribbed with silver tinsel and a wing of black squirrel hair. Make sure that when you tie off the hair that you cut its ends to a taper so that when the thread is wound over it you will get a smooth, tapering base on to which the deer hair can be spun. Some tyers use the cut-off end of a ball-pen to tap the fibres firmly down the hook shank before applying a further bunch of hair and this results in a very dense and tightly packed head which will increase the fly's buoyancy. The hollow hairs make deer hair a wonderful floatant.

BELOW: Clearing the way for additional applications of deer hair.

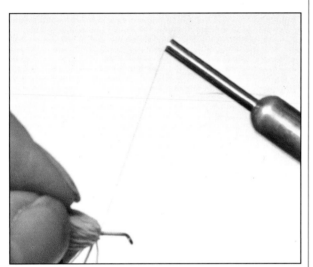

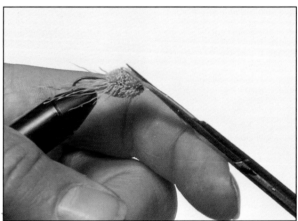

ABOVE: Muddler head clipped to shape.

LEFT: The finished muddler head.

ABOVE: A pair of hackles ready to make a streamer wing.

RIGHT: A streamer wing securely tied in.

STREAMERS

This technique involves using whole hackles tied in at the head of the fly to act as a wing and a long-shank hook is normally used. It is very important to check that the hackles to be used are identical in size and colour. Two are prepared by stripping the fluff from their base and then positioned so that their natural curves make their points come together rather like a pair of hands. The pair of feathers are then gripped in the left hand and tied on top of the hook as though they were a wing, using the pinch and loop technique. Additional security can be had by turning the stems back over themselves and tying down, this locks the hackles on.

RIGHT: Prepared hackles to make a matuka wing.

ABOVE: A matuka wing tied in.

MATUKAS

Very similar to the previous technique except that the body ribbing is left unwound while the hackles are put on as for the streamer. Very often the underside of each hackle is stripped off so that when laid down on to the shank the feathers look like a crest on top of the hook. Hold the tips of the hackles in the left hand and stroke the fibres back towards the eye so that they stand up away from the quill.

Now hold the hackle down on top of the hook and commence winding the ribbing material up over the hackles so that they are bound down on to the shank. Take great care to wind between the hackle fibres so that they do not become trapped and twisted out of shape. Finally, tie off the ribbing and stroke the fibres back down. Flies tied in this way tend not to tangle as do streamers when the wing bends down under the hook and gets trapped in the bend.

MARABOU

This is a very soft and fluffy feather which when wet is amazingly mobile in water. Used as tails up to 4-in long it pulsates and wiggles as the fly is retrieved and it makes excellent wings or bodies with lots of life. An easy way to prepare it for tying in for wing or tail is to cut a

LEFT: Ribbing to secure a matuka wing.

ABOVE: A shuttlecock of marabou fibres.

ABOVE: A marabou tail tied in.

section of fibres free from the main quill and to then wet the thumb and forefinger of your right hand and twist the ends of the fibres together so that they form what looks like a shuttlecock of fibres. These little 'shuttle-cocks' can then be tied in. Make a simple marabou fly by tying in a tail of black fibres then winding on a black chenille body and finally a black hen hackle. It might not look much but this pattern will catch fish the world over.

RIGHT: Winding on to achieve a dubbed body.

BELOW: Short fibred fur in a dubbing twister loop.

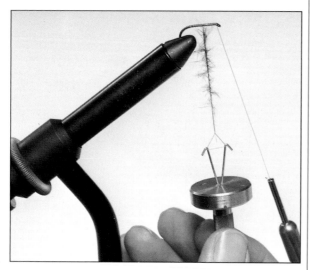

ABOVE: The twister spun to trap the fibres.

SHORT-FIBRED FURS

It is difficult to dub such material in the way I have previously described but a nice easy way is to use a dubbing twister. The idea is to have a loop of thread coming free of the body of the pattern and to hang the two loops of the twister from the thread loop. The fibres of fur are then carefully spread along the loop before the twister is spun. This twists up the thread loop and effectively traps the hairs. The twist can then be wound is just the same way as you wound the dubbing rope.

This technique does have the advantage over normal dubbing methods in that the hair fibres produce a more bulky effect and it is possible to adapt this to making a hair hackle by using guard hairs from some animals.

PARTRIDGE

These short feathers often cause a lot of trouble for fly tyers because they have a very thick base, so that if they are tied in by the base and wound round the hook they cause a lot of bulk. The correct thing to do is to stroke the fibres down from the tip to the base so that they stand out from the stem and to then tie in by the tip and wind the couple of turns necessary to get the hackle effect without having to get on to the thick part of the stem. The snag is that the feather is actually very weak and breaks easily, so it is a matter of carefully judging the amount of pressure to apply when winding the hackle.

WINGING WITH BODY FEATHERS

Wings of bronze mallard, wood duck or teal are an absolute nuisance to tie in as matched pairs because the fibres have very weak hook-and-eye systems to join them up and the whole lot will often fall apart as the pinch and loop is done. It is far better for all practical fishing purposes to stroke a section of fibres out at an angle to the stem so that the tips are all lined up and to them cut it away. The section of fibres is then folded in half and in half again before being placed between a wetted forefinger and thumb and rolled to and fro. This mixes up all the fibres to make what is called a rolled wing. This is then tied in as a whole section but still using the pinch and loop method.

BELOW: Bronze mallard feathers prepared for a bunched wing.

LEFT: Tying in a prepared partridge hackle.

CUTTING OFF DRY FLY HACKLES

It is very easy when cutting off the waste tip of a fully wound hackle for a dry fly to inadvertently cut away some of the fibres which you want. One way of overcoming this is to use your best scissors and open the points by just ¼ in. Keep the points open by this amount and then slide the hackle stem into the vee made by the blades. If you now either pull down on the hackle or push up with the scissors the stem of the hackle slides into the vee and is sliced through but only the tips are cut, not any of the fibres.

There are many more refinements and specialised techniques to fly tying and as I said in the opening pages the subject can be treated as an art form with tyers entering competitions to make the most technically perfect fly or the best imitative pattern. Fly tying can open up a whole new meaning to your understanding and enjoyment of the sport of fishing and if this book has set you on that road to taking your first fish on a fly of your own tying then I wish you a steady hand, nimble fingers and a never-ending queue of fish eager to take your offerings.

Fly tyers like to retain some record of their better achievements and a way of creating an attractive addition to the home is to set a collection of patterns into a frame and hang them on your wall. I made this set of salmon and trout flies for a very good friend and some are immensely complex but yet satisfying to tie. For example, the Jock Scott is true to its original tying and has 29 different sections of feather in its wing alone.

GLOSSARY

Abdomen: Segmented section of insect body. It does not bear legs but may have breathing filaments.

Badger: Term for colour of hackle feather, white-to-honey with black centre and tips.

Bobbin: Tool for retaining spool of thread under tension.

Caddis: Term for species of insect that makes a case to live in during the larval form. The adult is also often called a caddis fly.

Cape: The whole skin of a bird's neck up to the top of its head and complete with all the feathers.

Dubbing: Term used for the technique of applying hair to thread and then on to the body of the fly.

Dubbing needle: A needle set into a handle and used principally to pick out fibres from a dubbed body.

Ephemerid: A collective generic term for one of the largest groups of insects represented by the fly tyer.

Fibre: A single filament of feather.

Gape: The distance between the shank of a hook and the point.

Greenwell: Term for hackle colour, ginger with black centre.

Grizzle: Hackle colour, black and white barring.

Guard hair: The long hairs of a section of fur which actually are the show surface.

Hackle: Single feather from the cape or the feather when wound round the hook.

Hackle pliers: Spring-loaded tool used to grip a hackle when winding it round the hook.

Matuka: A style of dressing where the wing is bound down to the top of the hook-shank with turns of ribbing material.

Metz: Trade name for genetically reared feathers for fly tyers.

Neck: Another term for cape (which see).

Quill: The central stem of a feather or a whole feather, i.e. flight quill.

Shank: The length of a hook from the start of the bend up to the eye.

Streamer: Term for a style of dressing where the wings are long and made of hackle tied in at the head of the fly.

Thorax: The fatter part of an insect's body which carries the legs and from where the wings develop.

Tinsel: Metallic or lurex material used for ribbing or bodies.

Vice: The tool used to clamp the hook steady.

Jim Teeny with a magnificent
Chinook from Oregon.

INDEX

ACKNOWLEDGEMENTS

All photographs of techniques, materials and actual flies
by Andrew Stuart, © Quintet Publishing Limited 1990.
All photographs of fish and fishermen supplied by the
author.

ARC OF
THE GURKHA

ARC OF THE GURKHA

FROM NEPAL TO THE BRITISH ARMY

ALEX SCHLACHER

PRESENTED BY

First published 2014 by
Elliott and Thompson Limited
27 John Street, London WC1N 2BX
www.eandtbooks.com

ISBN: 978-1-90965-399-3

9 8 7 6 5 4 3 2 1

A catalogue record for this book is available from the British Library.

Design: Karin Fremer

Printed in China by 1010 Printing International Ltd.

To Ingrid – who taught me strength,
compassion and stubborn perseverance
and who loved this project even though
she never saw a single frame of it.

CONTENTS

INTRODUCTION

Brigadier Ian Rigden OBE (late Royal Gurkha Rifles)

I first met Alex Schlacher in late 2011. She approached me with the idea of producing a photographic record of Gurkha service when I was Colonel, Brigade of Gurkhas. Her idea had originated when she was photographing US Marines in Helmand Province, Afghanistan, and came across Gurkhas for the first time. Intrigued, she managed to spend a few weeks with them and was deeply impressed by their spirit. They were soldiers from my old battalion, 2nd Battalion The Royal Gurkha Rifles, under the command of Lieutenant Colonel Fraser Rea. Fraser and Major Jamie Murray, who was commanding B Company, with whom Alex spent most of her time, were so taken by her photographs that they sent me a selection and suggested that Alex and I should meet. Fraser also suggested that, with the 200th anniversary of Gurkha service to the British Crown on the horizon in 2015, a fresh look at the full spectrum of a Gurkha soldier's life in pictures would be invaluable.

Alex's commitment to this project has been exemplary. She has effectively put her life on hold for the last three years to bring this book to fruition. She has been given unprecedented access to Gurkha units and their soldiers at home, on operations and on exercise. That Alex cares passionately about Gurkhas is obvious by the quality of her images. She has lived alongside them, shared in their adventures and earned their respect. But it is the style and honesty of her photographs that lift this beyond just another photographic record. She has really connected with her subjects.

The first time I saw Alex's photographs, they were images of soldiers in the battalion I had commanded. They were my men, and to see their faces peering back at me as I remembered them brought back many wonderful memories and led to slightly watery eyes. But what really struck me was their obvious connection with Alex. They look directly at the camera, undaunted, proud and open in a way that I have seldom seen in other photographs of Gurkhas. These are honest and frank images that tell the story of an amazing lifelong journey – the physical act of being a Gurkha soldier. We are being given a glimpse of their humanity in all its glory and imperfection; every expression, smile, frown and line etched in their faces has an accompanying anecdote or message. Alex is not just a photographer, she is an artist, with all the passion, conviction, determination, skill and empathy with her subject that this one word invokes.

Alex has managed to project a vision of the lives of Gurkha soldiers from hopefuls, to joining, serving the British Crown, and into retirement. What she has effectively captured in images is one of our Brigade sayings: 'it is the Gurkha soldier that makes the Brigade, but it is the ethos and standards of the Brigade that make a Gurkha soldier' – a journey where the individual matters as much, and in fact more, than the institution he is joining. More importantly, she has also captured the fact that once a Gurkha soldier, these men will always be Gurkhas, whatever the length of their service. Being a Gurkha – whether soldier or officer, Nepali or British – shapes one's life for ever and this is clearly evident in her stunning photographic portraits.

The arc of a Gurkha is the trajectory of their careers as soldiers and is composed of a number of key events that make them Gurkhas and sustain their reputation for excellence. After selection and basic training, success and promotions open the way to further advancement through the attendance of career courses and other professional development up to the rank of Gurkha officer. It is important to note that all Gurkha officers are commissioned through the ranks, with the resultant maturity and experience that this brings, much of which is gained on deployments as well as during training.

Gurkhas have a significant story to tell and Alex captures this exceptionally well in this book. To put it into stark perspective, in the last fifteen years alone, many of the soldiers she has interviewed and photographed have served in Bosnia, Kosovo, Sierra Leone, Macedonia, the Congo, Iraq and Afghanistan. Of particular note,

at the time Alex was with the soldiers of B Company 2nd Battalion The Royal Gurkha Rifles in Helmand, over 50 per cent of the Company were on their fifth tour of duty in Afghanistan. It is what Gurkha soldiers join up to do, and they continue to live up to the highest standards of professionalism, commitment and comradeship.

Alex has also captured unit life and the part that it plays in shaping us. This is an area that is often neglected, but Gurkhas are a close-knit community, and their lives revolve around army and family life, and the balancing act that is required to meet both commitments.

At some stage all of us will leave soldiering, the profession we love, and will move on to pastures new. Again, Alex's images take us past active duty into retirement both in Nepal and increasingly the UK. She shows the importance that we place on providing for our soldiers in retirement, enabling them to live out their lives with dignity.

This is an exceptional book, with images of rare beauty. It is a very special contribution to the history of the Brigade but, most importantly, it is a labour of love that fully deserves the credits and accolades that it will undoubtedly accrue.

Jai Hos, Jai Gurkhali, Hami Jasto Kohi Chhaina!
(Hoorah all, hoorah the Gurkhas, there is nobody quite like us!)

A SHORT HISTORY OF THE BRIGADE OF GURKHAS

Brigadier Ian Rigden OBE

The name Gurkha is synonymous with courage, devotion and loyalty, moulded by the bond between Gurkha soldiers and their British officers. Whatever their cap badge, be it infantry, engineer, signaller, logistician or clerk, Gurkhas are all infantry first and shaped by the Rifle Regiment tradition. In 1966 Field Marshal Lord Bramall described the spirit of the Rifleman as: '. . . pride in fighting qualities and professional skill, intelligent and humane discipline, sympathy and understanding between all ranks and concern for the individual, for his welfare and for that of his dependants . . .'[1]

It is this fighting spirit, the importance of Nepalese culture and heritage and the bond between British and Gurkha officers and soldiers, that are the essence of the Brigade of Gurkhas. And it is underpinned by their belief in each other and the welfare of their soldiers and families.

A RICH TRADITION

Gurkhas have a natural cultural affinity with a number of other ethnic groups that often prevents violence and has been a real boon to British military capability in recent campaigns. However, it is for their physical fighting prowess in battle that Gurkhas are best known.

Gurkhas have only been eligible to receive the Victoria Cross, the highest military honour in the British Army, since 1911. Previously, those honours went to their British officers only. To date, twenty-six Victoria Crosses have been awarded to the Brigade: thirteen to Gurkha officers and soldiers, and thirteen to their British officers. Two Gurkha soldiers have also been awarded the George Cross for their life-saving work after the earthquake in Quetta, Pakistan, in 1933.

The arenas for these battles have been jungles, deserts, plains, rivers and mountains, in snow, rain, mud, cold and heat, all of which they have adapted to with skill and tenacity. Their enemies have been many and varied, including the Sikhs, Afghans, Malays, Germans, Turks, Japanese, Italians, Al Qaeda and the Taliban. Among these enemies, Gurkhas have always earned a great deal of respect. As time has gone by, many of these former enemies have become sworn friends and allies, but not all. The world remains a dangerous place and the Brigade of Gurkhas remains on standby to pre-empt hostility and react to the unexpected as an integral part of the British Army of the twenty-first century.

IN THE BEGINNING

Britain's friendship with Nepal and the lineage of the modern Brigade of Gurkhas can be traced back 200 years to 1815, making Nepal the UK's oldest ally in Asia. The journey began, however, not in friendship but in enmity, as the Army of Nepal clashed with the British East India Company when the latter tried to consolidate its hold on Northern India. As a result, the East India Company invaded Nepal in 1814. After two long and bloody campaigns, which were largely inconclusive, a

---

1 From a pamphlet written by Field Marshal Lord Bramall of Bushfield KG GCB OBE MC JP, 'Leadership The Green Jacket Way', 1966.

The 2nd Battalion 6th Gurkha Rifles in Baghdad, Mesopotamia (now Iraq) in 1917.

Undated image showing a British and a Gurkha officer of the 2nd King Edward VII's Own Gurkha Rifles (The Sirmoor Rifles) holding their former colours, carried between 1850 and 1863.

peace treaty was signed at Segauli in 1816. But it was between these campaigns, in April 1815, that the first Gurkhas, the Sirmoor Rifles, were recruited by Lieutenant Frederick Young in Nahan State. Young had been captured by Gurkhas during the campaign and had been so impressed with their martial qualities and general bearing that he knew they would be a great asset to the army of the East India Company. His views were quickly accepted by the other officers and soldiers and so began what is now known as the Brigade of Gurkhas.

SERVING THE EAST INDIA COMPANY AND THE RAJ
Although the Gurkhas started as a militia working for the East India Company, they later expanded and fought throughout India, including during the Sikh Wars of 1846 and 1848, and in the Indian Mutiny. It was during the latter that the steadfastness of the Sirmoor Battalion at Delhi, alongside their sister regiments, the 60th Rifles and Queen Victoria's Own Corps of Guides, earned the Brigade its Rifle Regiment tradition

of wearing a dark green uniform. It also won the unique accolade of the award of Nishanimai,[2] 'the mother of all battle standards', officially known as the Queen's Truncheon. It is a silver and brass standard, reputedly designed by Prince Albert, and unique because Rifle Regiments traditionally do not carry standards. The Sirmoor Battalion, as it was then called, under the command of Major Charles Reid, held the vital high ground overlooking Delhi for over three months. They repulsed twenty-seven major attacks of several thousand enemy fighters, allowing the Crown forces time to build enough strength to retake Delhi.

After the mutiny, the British Government took direct control of India from the Honourable East India Company, and the ensuing period between 1857 and 1947 became known as the British Raj. During the next fifty years, there was much active service for Gurkha units in Burma, Afghanistan, the frontiers of India, Malta, Cyprus, Malaya (now Malaysia), China (the Boxer Rebellion of 1900) and

---

2 *Nishan: standard; Mai: mother.*

Tibet. This period of Gurkha history was, however, mainly dominated by two cataclysmic events, the First and Second World Wars.

THE WORLD AT WAR

Some 200,000 Gurkhas served in the Indian Army during the First World War, of whom 8,000 were killed and 15,000 wounded in action. The regiments of the Gurkha Brigade fought and died in France and Flanders, Mesopotamia, Persia, Egypt, Gallipoli, Palestine and Salonika. A battalion of the 8th Gurkhas greatly distinguished itself at Loos, fighting to the last. The 6th Gurkhas also gained immortal fame at Gallipoli after a battle against the Turks to capture an area that later became known as 'Gurkha Bluff'. At Sari Bair they were the only troops in the whole campaign to reach and hold the top of the cliffs at Gallipoli.

There was little respite after the First World War, with fighting in the Third Afghan War in 1919 followed by numerous campaigns on the North-West Frontier, particularly in Waziristan. Four Nepalese Army regiments also took part in operations on the North-West Frontier during the Third Afghan War.

In the Second World War there were no fewer than forty Gurkha battalions in British service, as well as parachute, garrison and training units, totalling some 250,000 men. Of these, 15,000 were killed and 34,000 wounded in action. They fought and died side by side with British and Commonwealth troops, through victory and defeat, in the Western Desert, Italy and Greece, from North Malaya to Singapore and in Burma. The ties forged between those units are still very strong today.

Undated image of Gurkhas firing an anti-tank gun in North Africa during the Second World War.

THE TRANSFER TO THE BRITISH ARMY

Following the Second World War, there were conflicts in Palestine, the Dutch East Indies, French Indochina, Borneo and the troubled partition of India that claimed the attention and often the lives of officers and men of the Gurkha Brigade. But it was the start of Indian Independence on 15 August 1947 that ushered in a new era for the Brigade of Gurkhas and their ensuing involvement in the long process of the eventual British withdrawal from the whole of the Empire.

At the time of the partition of India, there were ten Gurkha regiments in the Indian Army, each consisting of a number of battalions. As a result of negotiations between the Nepalese, British and Indian Governments (known as the 'Tripartite Agreement') four of these regiments, each consisting of two battalions, were transferred to the British Army. Thus on 1 January 1948, four Gurkha regiments became, for the first time, an integral part of the British Army, forming the Brigade of Gurkhas. These regiments were: the 2nd King Edward VII's Own Gurkha Rifles (The Sirmoor Rifles), the 6th Gurkha Rifles, the 7th Gurkha Rifles and the 10th Gurkha Rifles.

When these regiments moved to the Far East in 1948, they were formed into a division along with other units of the British Army already there. As it was largely made up of Gurkhas, it was designated the 17 Gurkha Infantry Division. After 1948 the following additional Gurkha units were raised: Gurkha Engineers (now the Queen's Gurkha Engineers), Gurkha Signals (now the Queen's Gurkha Signals), Gurkha Army Service Corps (now the Queen's Own Gurkha Logistic Regiment), Gurkha Independent Parachute Company (disbanded in 1972) and Gurkha Military Police (disbanded in 1964). It is from these units that the modern Brigade of Gurkhas originates.

The Brigade of Gurkhas operated continuously throughout the Malayan Emergency. This was a twelve-year campaign (1948 to 1960) against Chinese communist terrorists whose aim was to overthrow the legitimate colonial government of Malaya. Gurkha soldiers again proved themselves to be superb jungle fighters. Whilst the majority of the rest of the British Army was fighting in other parts of the world, the Brigade of Gurkhas provided the backbone, the expertise and the continuity in the campaign, and they proved to be the decisive factor that led to victory in this vicious war of stealth and attrition, enabling Malaya to be an independent country.

Not long after that, Gurkha troops (1/2 GR) were again the first to be used in an operational role, this time during the outbreak of the Brunei Revolt in December 1962. The battalion was alerted at 11 p.m. on 7 December and the first company was air-landed in Brunei, 1,500 km (900 miles) away,

Soldier from 2 RGR in Kosovo, 1999.

at 9 a.m. the next morning. There followed four years of continuous operations against units of the Indonesian Regular Army in Sabah and Sarawak, in which every unit of the Brigade of Gurkhas took part. As they had done in the Malayan Emergency, Gurkha units again formed the main force of the British Army's contribution to this campaign.

THE DRAWDOWN OF THE BRIGADE OF GURKHAS

Between 1967 and 1972, as a result of changing defence commitments and the reorganisation of the Armed Forces, the strength of the Brigade of Gurkhas was reduced from 14,000 to about 8,000. When British forces withdrew from Singapore in 1971, a Gurkha Field Force was created in Hong Kong consisting of three Infantry Battalions, the Queen's Gurkha Engineers, the Queen's Gurkha Signals and the Gurkha Transport Regiment. Two further infantry battalions were based in Brunei and the UK, where they continue to serve to this day.

Despite their reduced numbers, the Gurkhas continued to play an important role in the British Army. In 1974, the 10th Gurkha Rifles (10 GR), the battalion based in England, deployed to Cyprus to reinforce the British Sovereign Base Area when Turkey invaded the Island. Further operations were conducted in Belize until 1993 and, in 1982, 1/7 GR took part in the Falkland Islands Campaign. In the Gulf War to liberate Kuwait in 1990/91, the Gurkha Transport Regiment provided the 28 (Ambulance) Squadron and the Band of the Brigade of Gurkhas deployed as stretcher bearers.

Following the Government's decision to reduce and restructure the Army, and the imminence of the British withdrawal from Hong Kong in 1997, the Brigade of Gurkhas reduced in size from 8,000 to 2,900 in 1998. In 1994, the four Rifle Regiments disbanded and were reformed into a large Regiment – The Royal Gurkha Rifles (RGR) – which initially consisted of three battalions, with his His Royal Highness The Prince of Wales as the Regiment's Colonel-in-Chief.

The Regiment was further reduced to two battalions in November 1996, on the withdrawal of 1 RGR from Hong Kong to the UK. At that time, three Gurkha Reinforcement Rifle Companies were formed to strengthen the British Infantry until 2005 when they were disbanded. In 2006 a further two were raised and served until they too were disbanded in 2012 and 2013, respectively. In 2011, the Brigade of Gurkhas reached its greatest strength since 1997, at 3,800. In line with the implementation of Army 2020 (the transformation of the British Army for the 2020s and beyond), the Brigade is again slated to reduce to 2,500 in 2015, the number that had originally been planned after the withdrawal from Hong Kong.

THE GURKHAS TODAY

The Brigade continues to play a full and active part in contemporary British military operations. Since 1998, units and sub-units of the Brigade at platoon level and above have deployed 104 times. Tours have included Bosnia, Kosovo, East Timor, Sierra Leone, Macedonia, the Congo, Iraq and Afghanistan. Gurkha units have been involved in Afghanistan since the beginning of the conflict. The RGR Battalions alone have deployed thirteen times between them in the last fourteen years, and the units have had elements on continuous active service.

The future remains uncertain, but it is hoped, as the British Armed Forces reconfigure for the challenges of the twenty-first century, that the connection with Gurkhas will long continue, and that through their actions and professionalism, they will always hold a place in the hearts of the British nation.

1

RECRUITMENT

The British Army recruits Gurkhas in Nepal once a year. The selection process is split up into two regional events, in the east and west, lasting around three weeks each, and successful candidates then proceed to the final, or central, selection. Each year, there are thousands of hopeful young men trying to gain one of only a handful of spots in the Brigade of Gurkhas. Only between 120 and 200 will succeed.

GURKHA RECRUITMENT for the British Army starts in early spring, with an announcement of the current selection criteria released to dedicated recruitment websites – a list of educational requirements, minimum and maximum age, height and weight parameters as well as the physical tests applicants are expected to perform at regional selection. A few months later, thousands of hopeful young Nepalese men between the ages of seventeen and a half and twenty-one travel to one of two British regional recruitment camps – Dharan for those from east Nepal and Pokhara for the westerners – for a day of tests.

Being a Gurkha is an enormous honour that most Nepalese boys aspire to, but for many families, having one or more members in the British Army is also the only way to secure a steady income substantial enough on which to survive. Families spend huge amounts of money training their sons (often paying training academies to do the job), some even take out loans. Boys train for months to pass selection, so not only is it a personal disappointment when they fail, but also a year of training and money spent in vain.

Starting at 4 a.m., the candidates for regional selection have their identity documents and school leaving certificates scrutinised, are searched for performance-enhancing substances, given a registration number, which is written on their chests and arms, and are then subjected to a series of medical, educational and physical tests. Failing just one at any stage of the process means immediate disqualification. Finally, the ones remaining in the game by mid-afternoon go through a bilingual personal interview, led by two Gurkha officers – one British, one Nepalese.

The registration numbers of the successful applicants from both regions are posted on the Internet a few weeks later and a lucky 400 candidates are called forward to central selection in Pokhara where they will again be subjected to rigorous testing. The three-week final selection process involves more detailed medical and educational exams, mental and physical agility challenges and the famous Doko Race – a 5-km (3-mile) endurance run while carrying a traditional Nepalese carrier basket, the 'doko', filled with 25 kg (55 lbs) of sand, up and down steep inclines and over rocky and unstable terrain.

A final interview concludes the selection process. The successful applicants are informed, the unsuccessful ones sent home, and a team of Gurkha section commanders and drill sergeants from the UK arrive to distribute uniforms, issue kit, and hold courses in military history, Western culture and Gurkha tradition. They also brief the new soldiers on the terms and conditions of their future service, and start practising drills with them.

After the official attestation parade, where they swear allegiance to the Queen, the new recruits travel to the UK to begin basic training.

Gurkha selection in 1902. A potential recruit's chest is measured, a practice still in place today.

Potential recruits during selection in 1960s Nepal. Gurkha recruitment for the British Indian Army (and, after 1947, the British Army) took place in India and then Malaya until the regional recruitment camps were established in Nepal in the early 1950s.

Recruits of the Gurkha Army Service Corps (now the the Queen's Own Gurkha Logistic Regiment) in 1959, at the Indian depot of Sungei Patani.

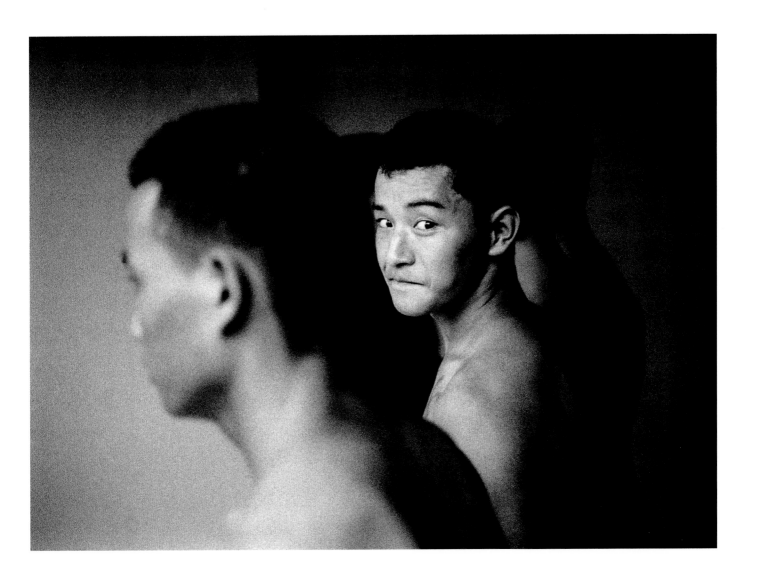

LEFT Potential recruits line up, their ages and individual registration numbers written on their chests, ready to begin a day of being measured, weighed as well as undergoing physical and medical tests during regional selection.

ABOVE Candidates wait to be called to the beam where they have to complete a minimum of twelve consecutive pull-ups in order to avoid failing this stage of the regional selection.

ABOVE Potential recruits wait to receive further instructions ahead of the next stages of selection.

RIGHT A candidate's chest is measured – boys with chests measuring less than 79 cm (31 in) are disqualified immediately.

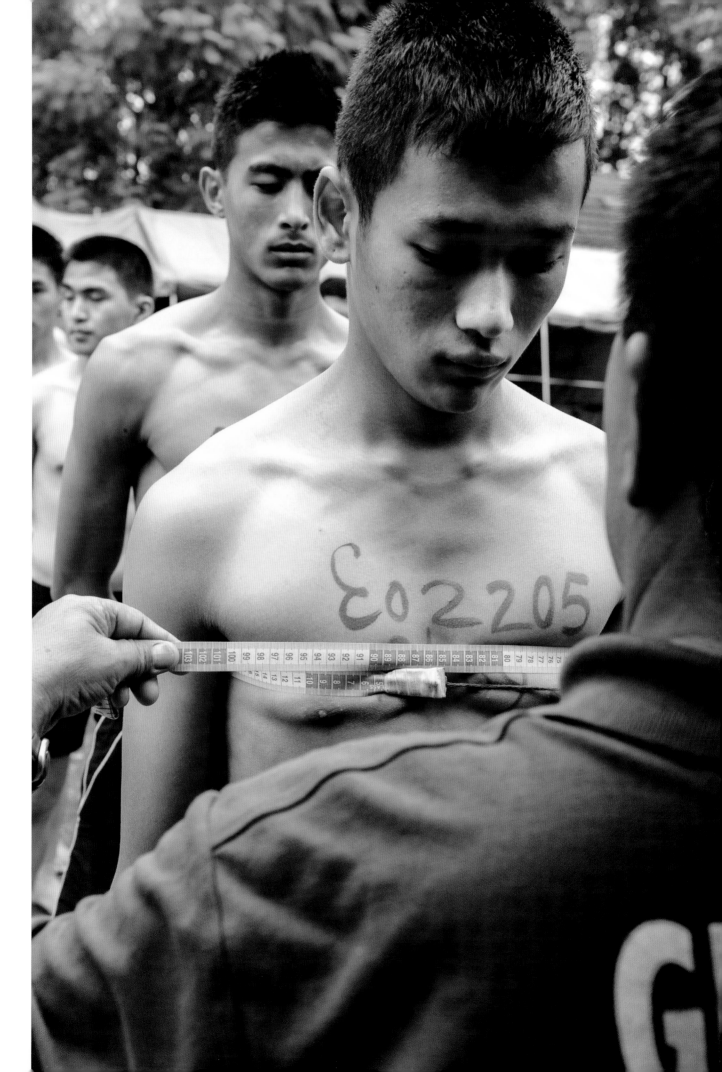

LEFT A potential recruit during the visual acuity test, supervised by one of the Gallas, retired Gurkhas employed to guide thousands of young Nepalese men through the selection process.

ABOVE Recruit Basanta Saud Thapa is the first man in his family to join the Gurkhas. He is also a 2nd Dan Black Belt in tae kwon do. He started practising the martial art when he was nine years old. By the time he was sixteen, he was already an instructor. Basanta was a member of the Nepalese national tae kwon do team and continued to practise the sport during selection and basic training.

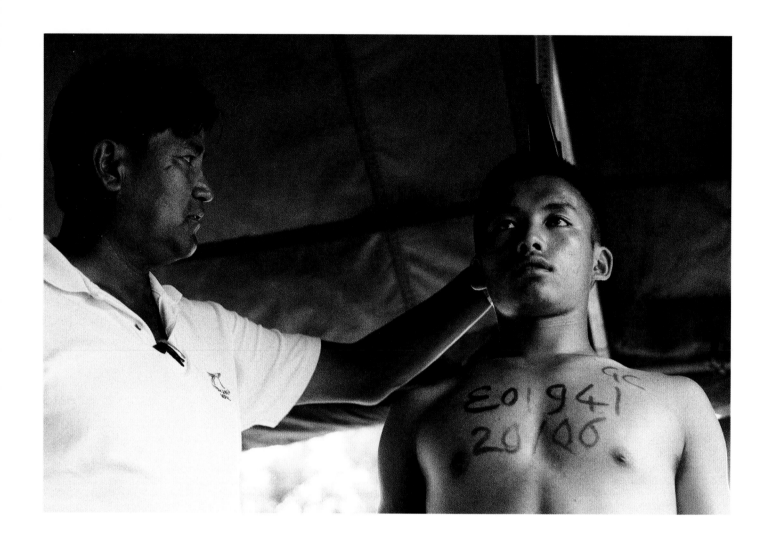

A candidate's height is measured. The minimum requirement is 158 cm (5 ft 2 in).

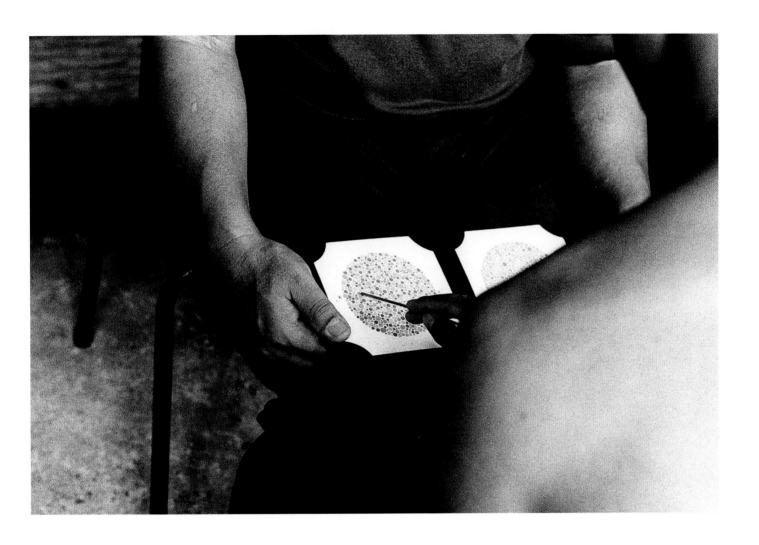

ABOVE During one of the test stages, potential recruits are subjected to the so-called Ishihara test to check for colour blindness. The candidate must be able to point out and trace a symbol or number within a pattern of dots of a different colour.

FOLLOWING PAGES Candidates stand to attention ahead of one of the written education tests.

ABOVE Even as a child, Recruit Abhishek Rajbhandari knew that he had to work hard to secure his future. Abhishek's mother left when he was just seven to work as a nanny in Israel and for the next seven years, he saw her only once. When his brother, who had been cooking and taking care of the family, left for Qatar to become a chef, Abhishek's father taught him how to survive and how to take care of his family, skills that he is now able to apply in the army.

RIGHT Recruit Nima Sange Sherpa was inspired to join the army by his brother, who is a soldier with the Royal Gurkha Rifles. He worked as a Sherpa guide all through his teens, assisting his father who had taken up the profession after retiring from the army. Nima loves the mountains and had already climbed to the Annapurna base camp by the age of fifteen.

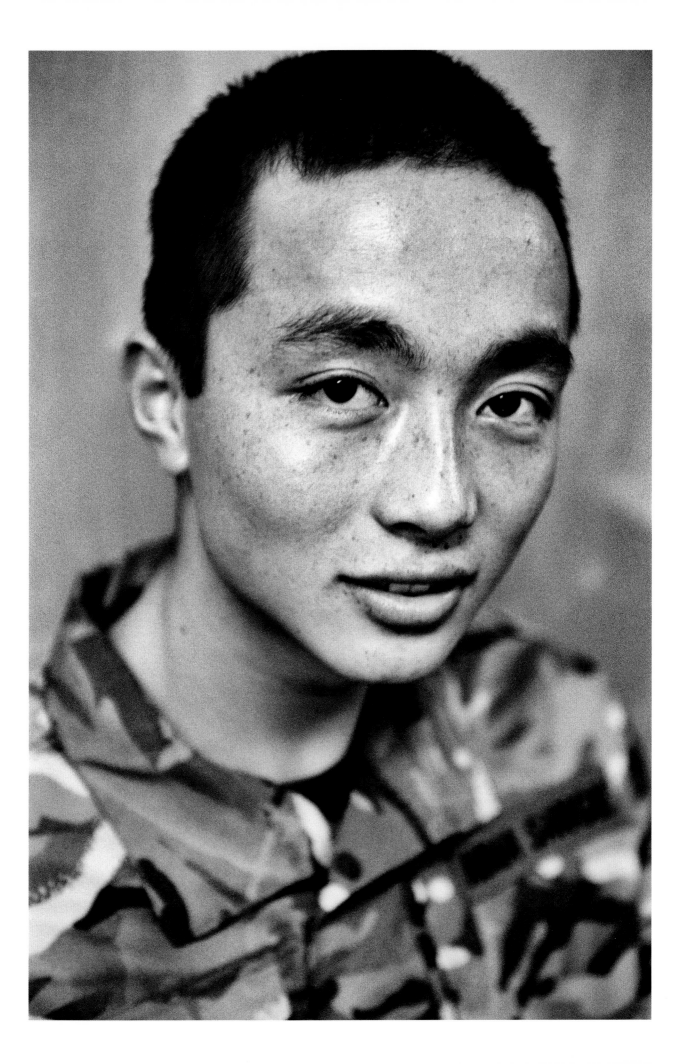

LEFT A potential recruit on the beam during the pull-up exam.

ABOVE Candidates start the 800-m sprint around the British Camp in Dharan, east Nepal, in the midday heat. It must be completed in under two minutes forty seconds.

ABOVE Recruit Sujan Limbu moved from Nepal to Darjeeling, India, at the age of four, as his father was a Gurkha in the Indian Army. He studied arts and humanities at college and spent much of his spare time with his aunt, an expert and instructor in what would become Sujan's great passion – rock climbing. Sujan represented India three times in international rock climbing championships, travelling to Japan, Kazakhstan and Iran, and won six gold medals at a national level.

RIGHT A candidate fighting through the required minimum of seventy sit-ups in two minutes, closely observed by a physical training instructor (PTI) who makes sure elbows are kept close to the body and the entire range of motion from ground to knees is completed.

Recruit Sandesh Rai was raised in an army family and played soldier from an early age – the only disadvantage to army life that he could see was being away from family and friends for long periods of time. Sandesh failed his first attempt at Gurkha selection due to poor eyesight but, determined to succeed, he saved up for eye surgery and was accepted on his second try.

Recruit David Ghising grew up with his grandparents. Originally he had wanted to be an engineer, but, as his family could not afford a university education, he decided to try for the British Army instead. He travelled to the British Camp in Dharan two days early out of fear that the impending general strike, a frequent occurrence in Nepal, might paralyse traffic and prevent him from getting to the regional selection on time. He just made it through the gate before it shut.

LEFT Recruit Prithvi Raj Rai's grandfather was in the British Army. Even before he joined, Prithvi had spent a lot of time thinking about the great responsibility that comes with being a soldier and the strange adjustment to the possibility of having to kill in combat. He went to the British Camp with a group of thirty-five friends and acquaintances to try out for the Gurkha selection. He was the only one of them who was accepted.

ABOVE Recruit Sanjaya Thapa was born in Singapore, but his family moved back to Nepal when he was five years old. His father was a member of the Singapore Police's Gurkha Contingent and he often told Sanjaya to try and make his family happier than he did himself, although Sanjaya had always been proud to be the son of a Singapore policeman. Now, after his successful admittance, his dad feels proud, in return, to be the father of a British Gurkha.

ABOVE A young Nepalese man on the first day of central selection in Pokhara, west Nepal. The mark on his forehead is called a tikka. It was put there by his parents for good luck.

RIGHT Candidates wait to begin the final written education test.

FOLLOWING PAGES A few hours of respite during central selection. Potential recruits can sign up for an optional swimming test. Many Nepalese boys do not know how to swim but, in the spirit of courage and initiative, they volunteer anyway. Most of them have to be rescued from drowning, spluttering and coughing, to the general amusement of their colleagues.

LEFT Candidates negotiate one of several mandatory command tasks – obstacle courses or challenges, requiring deductive as well as technical skills, that must be completed within a set time limit. These activities demonstrate teamwork as well as highlighting leadership qualities.

ABOVE Growing up with a very strict father taught Recruit Baghat Gurung perseverance. When he went over on his ankle a whole kilometre before the finish line during central selection's extremely tough Doko Race, he kept running, with the heavy basket on his back, ignoring the exploding pain in his sprained foot. He still finished three minutes faster than the maximum allowed time, coming in ahead of a number of his peers.

A young man prepares his basket for the demanding Doko Race.

Potential recruits during the Doko Race. The steep track runs up uneven steps, over boulders, up slippery gravel roads and through forest areas, and has to be completed in forty-eight minutes or less carrying a basket filled with sand. Each candidate's doko is weighed before and after the race to prevent cheating.

ABOVE Recruit Harkajang Limbu comes from a small village in east Nepal that still does not have reliable electricity or running water. While he was training for Gurkha selection, Harkajang volunteered at a school for the blind. His cousin and uncle are also British Army Gurkhas and so was his great-grandfather, who died in the Burma campaign of the Second World War. Sadly, his family does not have any pictures or service medals to remember him by.

RIGHT Recruit Surya Prakash Limbu, from east Nepal, grew up in a middle class family and wanted to be a Gurkha ever since he can remember. He has passionate opinions, particularly about politics and human rights. He occasionally argues with one of his brothers about religion, but has wisely come to the conclusion that just because two people believe in different things, that does not mean either one of them is wrong.

PREVIOUS PAGES Gurkha recruits line up for a tae kwon do lesson a few days after passing central selection.

ABOVE Potential recruits negotiate a command task – one designated leader has to direct each member of his blindfolded team to a certain spot in a large square using only non-verbal cues such as whistling or drumming.

RIGHT Nervous candidates wait to be called for their final interview during central selection on a cold December morning in Pokhara.

ABOVE One of the section commanders from the Infantry Training Centre in Catterick, UK, where new recruits go for nine months after being selected, adjusts a successful candidate's beret. Section commanders are like substitute fathers to the young men starting basic training, most of whom are experiencing life away from their parents for the first time.

RIGHT One of the first items on a new Gurkha recruit's itinerary: the mandatory haircut.

LEFT AND ABOVE New recruits during their daily physical training lesson incorporating running, tae kwon do and interval training.

Recruit Suman Chandra Gahatraj grew up in a small village in west Nepal. The caste system is still prevalent in many parts of Nepal and Suman's caste has traditionally produced bankers and gold traders. He is the first from his extended family ever to join the army, a very unusual career path for him to choose. The day he was accepted into the Gurkhas was the most significant in his life – he still remembers the exact time he was told he had made it.

Recruit Samso Wanem Phago grew up in east Nepal and Kathmandu. Before he joined the Gurkhas, Samso played guitar and sang in a band. His grandfather, two uncles and two brothers are soldiers, and although his parents attempted to steer him towards an engineering degree, he convinced them to let him try out for the British Army. He got in on the first attempt.

New recruits during drill practice. Section commanders coach them to master the precise
angles of head, arms and hands required to perform a parade march.

Gurkha recruits swear allegiance to Britain and a portrait of Queen Elizabeth II during their attestation parade.

For each intake, British Gurkhas Pokhara hosts a celebration, inviting the successful candidates' parents and siblings, who travel from all over Nepal, bringing gifts and food. At that point the new Gurkha recruits have had no contact with their loved ones for weeks and, seeing their proud and very emotional parents for the first time after passing selection, many of the boys, whose newfound employment will safeguard their family's future, are lost for words.

ABOVE Ahead of the trip to a new life in the UK as Gurkha recruits, the eight-hour bus ride from the British Camp to Nepal's capital, Kathmandu, provides time for a little reflection and a lot of sleep.

FOLLOWING PAGES New Gurkha recruits meet Gurkha veterans at a retirement home for soldiers, run by the Gurkha Welfare Trust in the west Nepal district of Kaski.

BASIC TRAINING

Gurkha basic training starts in Nepal, immediately after the new recruits are selected. Two weeks later, they travel to the UK for nine months of physical training, weapons handling and tactics as well as further education, language courses and cultural immersion. Basic training culminates in the so-called passing-out parade, after which the new trainee riflemen join their individual regiments.

THE BRIGADE OF GURKHAS was based in Hong Kong until 1997. Soldiers recruited before then remember, in particular, harsh training conditions and the huge culture shock of moving from hill villages in Nepal to Hong Kong, a city that seemed like a futuristic metropolis to them.

When the Brigade moved to the UK, basic training facilities were located in Church Crookham, Hampshire, and subsequently in Catterick, North Yorkshire, where they remain to this day.

In the first few weeks of basic training, in order to focus the new batch of recruits, now called trainee riflemen, access to phones or the Internet is not allowed. Lessons in military theory, as well as basic skills like polishing boots, ironing and cleaning, to which they were introduced during their last weeks at the recruitment camp in Nepal, are expanded on.

Basic training also consists of drills, physical training and outdoor exercises that teach each unit of fresh Gurkhas how to survive in nature and how to build harbours, rain roofs and barricades. Recruits are taught the use and care of their uniforms, equipment and rifles as well as first aid and casualty evacuation procedures. They learn how to operate in sections, patrolling as well as attacking and retreating from targets. Finally, they are taken on excursions across the UK to learn about the country's history and culture. Both Nepali and English are spoken during basic training, and while these trainee riflemen are immersed in a completely new environment in every aspect of their lives, the staff at the Infantry Training Centre take care to surround them with Nepalese food, music and the celebration of traditions like Dashain, the Nepalese equivalent of Christmas.

At around the six-month point, after attending presentations from all the Gurkha Brigade's units, the young men are asked to pick their top three regiments. Their preferences will be taken into account, but are not guaranteed. A few weeks before the end of basic training, they receive their cap badges – the symbol of their enrolment in the regiment they will serve for the rest of their careers.

There are competitions dotted throughout the nine months the recruits spend in Catterick. Champion recruits for individual regiments are crowned as well as the overall champion of each year's intake and, at the end of basic training, the new riflemen celebrate the successful completion of their military training in the passing-out parade.

From there, the young men who join corps units, the clerks or the Band go on to advanced training facilities while the riflemen joining one of the two infantry units immediately travel to their respective battalions to begin work.

The normal drop-out rate of recruits during basic training within the British Army is around one third. In the Brigade of Gurkhas, it is zero.

Rifle lesson during basic training, India, 1890s.

Basic training in Hong Kong in the 1970s.

Physical training session for new recruits, India, ca 1950s.

ABOVE Rifleman Tej Kumar Paija was born in India and moved back to Nepal when he was eight years old. He grew up admiring a picture of his father, a soldier in the Indian Army, crouching on the ground surrounded by an icy desert somewhere in Kashmir, carrying a rifle. He was so fascinated with soldiers that he collected shell casings, ran military obstacle courses with friends for fun and started to exercise with older boys who were training to join the British Army. Tej is now a member of the Royal Gurkha Rifles (RGR) and is currently stationed in Brunei.

RIGHT Trainee riflemen negotiating a combat exercise track during basic training.

LEFT A new recruit polishing his boots.

ABOVE Sapper Rupesh Gurung comes from Gorkha, the district in northern Nepal that gave the Gurkhas their name. Conversations with his grandfather, a soldier in the Nepalese Armed Forces, inspired him early on in life, but he also had a fascination with genetics and studied science for a while before trying out for the British Army. He was the top engineering recruit during basic training and has since joined the Queen's Gurkha Engineers.

FOLLOWING PAGES The training programme for new recruits includes tabbing – marching over long distances carrying a large amount of kit.

ABOVE Private Vivek Gharti is from a village in a largely industrial area near the Indian border, and he speaks and writes Hindi fluently. There were never any Gurkhas in his family and his parents had a university education in mind for him – Vivek himself was interested in medicine – but his grandmother suggested the army, an option he hadn't considered before, so he gave it a try and succeeded. He says that even during his short time in the military so far, he has grown more as a person than he could ever hope to as a civilian. Vivek is now with the Gurkha Staff and Personnel Support Company.

RIGHT Shooting practice is an almost daily occurrence during basic training, at both indoor and outdoor ranges.

ABOVE AND RIGHT Trainee riflemen, split up into sections, are tasked with clearing houses that contain explosives and enemy fighters (the explosives being harmless smoke bombs and the enemy fighters played by instructors). These exercises teach the new recruits how to operate under pressure and in a team.

ABOVE A long march in full combat gear during an exercise in Brecon, Wales.

RIGHT Rifleman Hari Rai comes from a very small village in the Khotang district of east Nepal. He finished school a year ahead of his peers, worked as a private science tutor and studied microbiology in Dharan before joining the Gurkhas. The British Army enabled him and his colleagues to experience many things for the first time during cultural excursions, which are part of the curriculum, such as seeing the ocean and making a journey on an underground train. After basic training, Hari joined the RGR.

FOLLOWING PAGES Trainees during an exercise near their training base in Catterick, learning how to camouflage their equipment and skin.

ABOVE Private Suraj Limbu grew up aware of the injuries his grandfather, a retired Gurkha for the British Army, had suffered in combat. He felt a great responsibility to continue the family history so he sacrificed his dream of becoming a professional football player and joined the army. Suraj is now with the Queen's Own Gurkha Logistic Regiment. He believes his journey as a soldier with the Brigade of Gurkhas will show him who he is.

RIGHT Recruits regrouping for an attack during a tactical exercise in Brecon, Wales.

LEFT Recruits help each other climb up a 3-m (9-ft) wall during combat physical training.

ABOVE Practical manoeuvres during exercises are interspersed with briefings on tactics and intermittent evaluations.

ABOVE Trainee riflemen during the traditional 13-km (8-mile) run, carrying rifles and full backpacks.

RIGHT A new recruit waiting to climb across an obstacle consisting of metal bars and ropes. Negotiating hurdles and walls at speed in full military kit is initially awkward, and is therefore practised frequently.

LEFT A popular class among young recruits is rifle assembly, in which different parts of the weapon, as well as various pieces of ammunition, are demonstrated and explained in detail.

ABOVE Rifleman Ajaya Tamrakar attempted and failed Gurkha selection three times, a severe blow to him and his family each time. But, unwilling to give up, Ajaya got in eventually through sheer determination and hard work. He proceeded to become champion recruit of his 126-strong intake in 2013 and has since joined the RGR.

FOLLOWING PAGES Climbing the 2-m (6-ft) wall is not one of the recruits' favourite activities. The goal is to jump up and climb over it, rifle slung across the back.

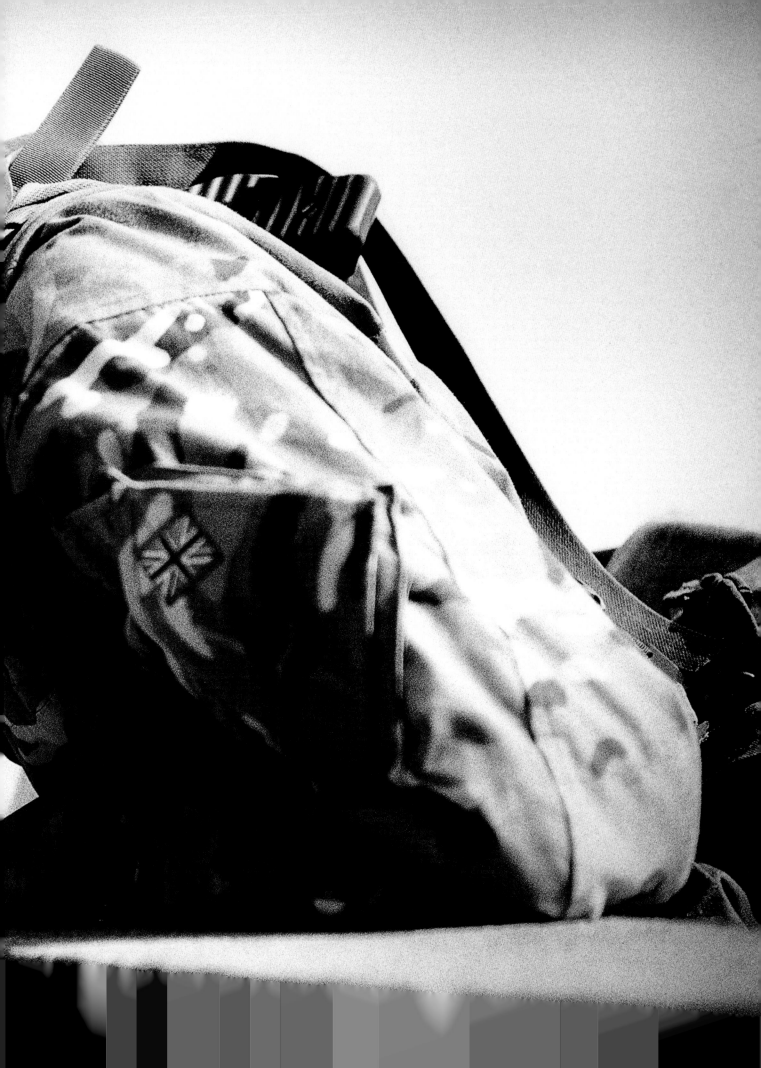

LEFT Private Suresh Dewan comes from an army background but, for a long time, was very focused on studying. He was the top student and school captain, showed an interest in civil engineering and was working on a bachelor's degree in science when he decided to join the army instead, in order to support his family. Suresh, like most of his peers, is very aware of the significance of the Brigade he is now a part of, and is therefore conscious of the fact that his actions and words represent much more than just himself. He has joined the Gurkha Staff and Personnel Support Company.

ABOVE Signaller Dirgha Raj Gurung grew up in Singapore in a culturally diverse environment, an experience he values very much, and he attended schools in both Kathmandu and India. When he joined the British Army, he realised his childhood dream of becoming a soldier. When asked what he would do if he had a lot of money, he said he would give it all away to people more in need of it than himself. Having completed basic training, Dirgha joined the Queen's Gurkha Signals.

ABOVE Rifleman Yam Kumar Rai grew up in a remote village in the Khotang district of east Nepal. His family is made up of eight members; the adults mostly work as farmers and teachers. Yam's income is virtually all the money the family has, so even during basic training, he sent almost 80 per cent of his monthly £900 salary back home to Nepal so his family could afford food, clothes and schooling for the other children. He is proud to be a Gurkha and to be able to secure his family's future. Yam has joined the RGR.

RIGHT Trainee riflemen at the Catterick Infantry Training Centre during a tae kwon do introductory class. Several of the recruits already have moderate to expert knowledge in martial arts.

ABOVE AND RIGHT Recruits and training staff participating in the Dashain festival at the training centre in Catterick. Dashain is the most important holiday in Nepalese culture and is celebrated across the Brigade of Gurkhas. There are a number of religious as well as martial traditions observed over a period of several days, like the ritual slaughter of goats and buffalo. In the UK, the animals are substituted with very large cucumbers. The soldier tasked with the slaughter of the animal or vegetable is then covered in red paint and given small sums of money. It is a tradition believed to bring good fortune.

LEFT Daily physical exercise is an essential part of the basic training programme and includes circuit training, swimming, endurance runs, sprint competitions, tae kwon do and stretching.

ABOVE Before the new recruits receive their own khukris, the Gurkhas' legendary machete-like knives, they practise with wooden substitutes.

Wearing their dress uniforms, trainee riflemen line up to perform a final rehearsal for the passing-out parade, the ceremony that concludes nine months of basic training and is attended by the recruits' families, who travel all the way from Nepal to see their sons become fully fledged Gurkhas of the British Army.

SERVICE

Today's Brigade of Gurkhas consists of several regiments – the three corps regiments are the Queen's Gurkha Engineers, the Queen's Gurkha Signals and the Queen's Own Gurkha Logistic Regiment. The infantry regiment, the Royal Gurkha Rifles, is split into two battalions, 1 RGR and 2 RGR. In addition, there are the Gurkha Staff and Personnel Support Company, the training support companies Sittang Company and Mandalay Company, and the Band of the Brigade of Gurkhas. The number of serving Gurkhas in the British Army has fluctuated over the years and currently stands at around 2,500.

IN PUBLIC PERCEPTION, the Gurkha infantry is the basis of the Gurkha legend. It is what people imagine when they hear of Gurkhas in combat. These infantry soldiers have been fighting at the front lines of most of the British and Indian Armies' key campaigns since 1815. But they have also been tasked with mentoring and peacekeeping, as well as security and reconstruction roles. The Brigade of Gurkhas does not just consist of infantry troops, however, but also of a number of corps regiments, each with its own very individual history, whose members perform a range of specific duties.

In 1870, the first Telegraph Battalion in the British Army was formed within the Corps of Royal Engineers, though it would be almost sixty years before the first official Signals Corps was created in 1921. The first recorded posting of Gurkha signallers was in the year 1911. They came from within three Indian engineering and mining corps units and turned into entire companies of specialised signallers during the First World War. After the Second World War, a signals unit for a specific Gurkha infantry division was created. It was called the X Brigade and formed the basis of what would become a modern Gurkha Signals Regiment. They received their official badge in 1954, became the Gurkha Signals the following year and were awarded the royal title of Queen's Gurkha Signals (QG Signals) in 1977.

The first Gurkhas joined the Royal Engineers in 1948. After going through several changes of title, role and designation, the Gurkha Engineers, as they were called at the time, were officially

Naik (Corporal) Agansing Rai of the 5 GR (Frontier Force), recipient of the Victoria Cross, the highest military honour in the British Army, for his actions in Burma in the Second World War.

formed, receiving their own cap badge and insignia. In 1977, the name was again changed to the Queen's Gurkha Engineers (QGE), after being awarded the royal title by Her Majesty Queen Elizabeth II.

In 1858, the Gurkha Army Service Corps was formed to provide transport and logistic support to the Gurkha Division based in Malaya. In 2001, after going through a number of changes and having been awarded a royal title, they became the Queen's Own Gurkha Logistic Regiment (QOGLR).

Finally, there are also Gurkha Company Sittang and Gurkha Company Mandalay, the two training support units of the Brigade of Gurkhas, formed in 1972 and 1974, respectively; the Gurkha Staff and Personnel Support Company (GSPS), which was formed in 2011, their duties previously having been performed by a unit called the Gurkha Clerks; and the Band of the Brigade of Gurkhas, which was raised in its earliest form in 1859 as part of a Gurkha Regiment of the Indian Army.

Gurkha paratroopers, part of the 44th Indian Airborne Division, British Indian Army, 1945.

Gurkha Signals wireless operator, Malaysia, ca 1960s.

Two QGE sappers operating a drill on Rompin Road, Malaysia, ca 1960s.

Soldiers of the Gurkha Transport Regiment hooking equipment loads to a helicopter in Malaysia, 1966.

TRAINING AND DEVELOPMENT

Once a new Gurkha recruit has completed basic training and has joined his regiment, he continues to strive for advancement. Competition for promotion among peers within the regiments is intense and starts with the Junior Leadership Cadre (JLC), which is the make-or-break point for a full career, as failure means potentially being stuck in a low rank for a very long time, which in turn can shorten a military career considerably. The advance training and exams that lead to promotion are taken as an opportunity to improve skill sets and expertise throughout a Gurkha career. Almost all Gurkhas want to become officers, and nowadays more and more of them achieve that goal.

Riflemen of the RGR listen to a strategy class during their JLC at a training area near the edge of the jungle in Brunei. A top grade in the JLC means a fast promotion to Lance Corporal.

PREVIOUS PAGES Soldiers line up for a final team photograph at the end of an exam.

LEFT AND ABOVE Soldiers of all regiments constantly hone their combat skills, such as tactics and casualty evacuation, and are regularly tested on them.

LEFT AND ABOVE Leadership skills are polished from the moment a Gurkha joins his regiment. Early on in the soldiers' careers, they learn how to lead small troop sections and, later on, entire platoons in battle.

FOLLOWING PAGES Foot patrols are a regular task on deployments and are performed nearly every day. A soldier's vigilance, eye for detail and speedy reactions are essential skills that need to be acquired and frequently practised.

ABOVE AND RIGHT The RGR is a light-role infantry, which means that the soldiers don't have vehicles or heavy equipment, enabling them to move fast. But even the bare minimum of weaponry, rations and essential materials that an infantry soldier carries in battle is quite heavy, so exercises are always completed in full combat gear to keep the situation as realistic as possible.

Section commander of a training unit during a JLC.

The stretcher race is an endurance test. Participants work in teams, running while carrying weighted stretchers, thereby simulating a casualty evacuation at speed and over difficult terrain like boulders or sand.

LEFT Courses and exams always include setting up harbours – secure areas where troops can overnight – and cooking military rations. There are 24-hour and 12-hour ration packs that include calorie-rich ready meals and energy snacks.

ABOVE During infantry courses, designated training sections demonstrate the correct way of approaching an enemy target as well as different types of attack and retreat.

ABOVE During exams, small sections of soldiers are given a challenge or a task and are then left to their own devices to figure out a solution. Some soldiers employ visual aids such as coloured chips to illustrate their strategy.

RIGHT Soldier throwing a grenade at a target during a JLC.

BAND OF THE BRIGADE OF GURKHAS

Military bands have always been a part of army life. The earliest recorded occurrence of army bands is from the Ottoman Empire, but it is very likely that they existed long before then, and that musicians have been used to call soldiers to duty and escort them into combat ever since mankind's earliest wars.

Originally, military bands served at the front lines to raise morale and to direct the movements of troop units in the loud, chaotic environment of an open battlefield. They also served as stretcher-bearers, mostly unarmed, carrying their wounded and dying colleagues to safety, as advancing troops were not allowed to stop and care for their casualties. During the 19th century, military bands started taking on a more ceremonial role, playing at dinners, funerals, parades and as general troop entertainment, although they continued to serve as stretcher-bearers as recently as the First Gulf War.

Musicians are recruited to the Band of the Brigade of Gurkhas after completing basic training. They initially receive four years of instruction in musical theory as well as their designated instruments and later go on to advanced training at the Royal Military School of Music in London. Today, in addition to playing regularly at regimental parades, the Band travels extensively all over the world, introducing Gurkhas to a global audience.

PREVIOUS PAGE The Brigade Band playing at the new Gurkha recruits' attestation parade in Pokhara, Nepal.

ABOVE Growing up in east Nepal, Corporal Kiran Mukhiya was always a keen football player and for a long time was aiming to play for the national team. Instead, he gave the army a try in 1998 and was selected for the Brigade Band. After a foundation course in musical theory, he started playing the trombone. With the Brigade Band, Kiran has travelled further than any of his colleagues in other regiments, having visited Germany, Cyprus, Canada, the USA, France, Bosnia, Brunei, Austria and even Pakistan. Kiran is extremely proud to have played concerts for international audiences and to represent the Gurkhas through music all over the world.

RIGHT There are bagpipers in every unit of the Brigade of Gurkhas. At important events, like the passing-out parade in Catterick, they join the Brigade Band.

ABOVE The Band of the Brigade of Gurkhas consists of musicians playing every type of instrument – brass, wind, string and percussion. A number of band members are also experts in traditional Nepalese music and know how to play various flutes and drums mainly used in Nepal.

RIGHT Corporal Krishna Bahadur Tamang, raised in west Nepal, was recruited into the Gurkhas in 1998. Growing up, he had been very musical, regularly singing as well as playing the flute and the Madal, a traditional Nepalese hand drum. He even recorded a pop album with his band that made it into the national charts. After joining a music college in Nepal, he tried out for the British Army on a whim, was accepted and immediately volunteered to join the Brigade Band. After his basic course, he began playing the trumpet, trying to emulate his idol Louis Armstrong. When the Brigade Band plays the regimental march or travels to support the Brigade and lift morale, Krishna feels he is where he belongs.

GURKHA STAFF AND PERSONNEL SUPPORT COMPANY

The GSPS is responsible for human resources, providing administrative and financial support to the entire Brigade of Gurkhas and beyond.

In the old days of Galla or hill recruitment, the recruiters would tour the Nepalese hinterland looking for potential Gurkha candidates, selecting boys who seemed well educated and displayed a firm grasp of general knowledge as potential technical recruits or clerks. Until around the Second World War, those selected for clerk posts tended to be the sons of serving Gurkhas, as they had grown up on military bases and therefore had a superior level of education. However, following the Tripartite Agreement (see page 14), each newly formed Gurkha battalion had its own clerical wing and the Brigade began recruiting clerks mainly from Gurkha communities in India.

GSPS staff now serve at Brigade Headquarters and are attached to each Gurkha regiment, deploying on operations as well as exercises.

A Gurkha clerk of the GSPS reconciling data in a makeshift field office during an exercise in Kenya.

ABOVE Corporal Rakam Thamshuhang spent the first few years of his life at the British Army base in Brunei – both his father and uncle had had long careers in the British Army. The family moved back to Nepal when he was four and initially struggled hard to find their foothold – for a while they even moved the entire extended family of fifteen children and several adults to a hostel. Rakam described himself as a bit lost as a teenager and had been heading down a worrying path before he pulled himself together and finished school. He worked at a call centre to support himself while he was studying for a BA in business administration, and to take care of his sick father, but eventually joined the army in 2008, believing it was what he was meant to do. While he was in basic training, Rakam received the news that his father had died and he finished his training in a haze of grief. He has since served as a clerk attached to one of the Gurkha infantry regiments as well as Brigade HQ.

RIGHT Corporal Anil Thapa grew up in Dharan, east Nepal, and started studying microbiology at college after graduating from secondary school. There are no Gurkhas in his extended family and Anil's dream was to become a doctor. However he worried greatly about his family's financial means and wanted his younger sister to have a proper education, so in 2005 he made a decision to try for the British Army instead. Anil served a tour in Afghanistan, where he tried to find an outlet to cope with the pressures of combat by running a half-marathon inside the camp almost every day. He is currently working as a military clerk at Brigade HQ.

LEFT Warrant Officer class 2 (WO2) Khadak Bahadur Chhetri grew up in an environment steeped in Gurkha culture and developed a strong desire to emulate his forefathers' honourable careers. His father served in Borneo in the 1960s and his grandfather, a local hero who was responsible for bridge- and road-building projects in his village in west Nepal, fought in both world wars, receiving a Military Cross for bravery in combat. Khadak joined the British Army in 1992, beginning a very successful career as a military clerk. He served in Bosnia and twice in Afghanistan before being posted to Brigade HQ. He has recently returned from a third tour in Afghanistan as a financial and administrative mentor to Afghan Special Forces Units and has been awarded the Meritorious Service Medal by Her Majesty Queen Elizabeth II.

ABOVE Staff Sergeant Sumit Joshi's grandfather, brother and three uncles all became soldiers, which largely influenced his decision to try for the British Army in 1998. When he was accepted, he gave away his shoes and clothes to a couple of distraught boys who had failed selection and needed cheering up. Sumit served in Kosovo both as an infantryman and a clerk. After a stint as a pay clerk at the Infantry Training Centre in Catterick, he had the huge honour of becoming the personal orderly of His Royal Highness The Prince of Wales for two years. Sumit also served in Afghanistan twice as one of the soldiers handling compassionate issues and casualty paperwork for bereaved families – a daunting task when the concerned individuals were strangers, but even more so when his best friend was killed in action. Sumit is currently posted to Brigade HQ.

TRAINING SUPPORT COMPANIES

There are two Gurkha training support companies within the British Army: Sittang Company in Sandhurst and Mandalay Company in Brecon, Wales. Both consist of chosen soldiers from all regiments of the Brigade who serve an average of two years with the training companies.

Sittang Company started in 1972 and, having gone through various changes, was officially set up in its current form in 1981, part of the Royal Military Academy in Sandhurst (RMAS). It is named after the Second World War battle of Sittang Bridge in Burma. The 140 members of this company provide security as well as administrative support to the RMAS and assist in cadet training by playing the role of the enemy during combat exercises and demonstrating battle manoeuvres. They also participate in endurance races for charity, raising money for the Gurkha Welfare Trust as well as local communities, and in shooting and military patrolling competitions.

Mandalay Company, also named after a battle that took place in Burma during the Second World War, has been based in Wales since 1974 and was formally set up in 1980. It supports the Infantry Battle School in Brecon by providing training and guidance as well as playing the part of the opposing force during exercises and exams. It was recently reduced from 124 members to 45 due to budget cutbacks.

RIGHT Sittang Company soldiers get ready for a tactical demonstration during a class for officer cadets at the Royal Military Academy in Sandhurst.

LEFT Captain Mahendra Phagami joined the Gurkhas in 1993 and was initially sent on operations to Kosovo and Bosnia. He was trained to detect and decontaminate nuclear, biological and chemical weapons. During his career, he worked as a jungle warfare instructor in Brunei and served in Afghanistan twice. On the second of those two tours, he was severely injured during a mortar attack while on a mission and found himself on the ground in the kill zone in the middle of a heavy firefight, unable to move for an hour. He couldn't see much but was able to hear the entire battle – shouting and rounds flying overhead – and when his unit finally managed to extract and evacuate him, he had almost lost too much blood to survive. He just made it to the hospital, and from there started a long road to recovery, battling hard to stay positive. Unable to remain idle at home for long, he asked to be reinstated as soon as possible and was eventually posted to Gurkha Company Sittang. He is a top golf player and has won several international cups for injured service personnel, most recently the Courage Cup against US veterans.

ABOVE A member of Sittang Company scouts various training locations during an exercise in Dumfries and Galloway, Scotland.

FOLLOWING PAGES Playing the role of the enemy is a large part of the job for both Sittang and Mandalay companies and presents a welcome challenge.

LEFT Corporal Raj Rai was born in east Nepal and raised in Singapore, where his father was based as a member of the Gurkha Contingent of the Singapore Police. He was a good student and grew up learning and speaking Nepalese, Mandarin Chinese, English and Malay. Raj was working as a sound and lighting engineer after graduation when his father convinced him to try out for the British Army. He trained hard for the selection, particularly the Doko Race – lacking any opportunity to practise running up hills in Singapore, Raj packed dumbbells into a backpack and sprinted up and down high-rise buildings. He passed selection with ease and joined the RGR in 2004, serving three tours in Afghanistan. His most enduring memories from these deployments are not being able to shower for weeks, as the water was being saved for drinking, and being attacked with grenades and RPGs every single day while bunkered down in a compound. Raj completed a four-year posting with Gurkha Company Mandalay in 2014 and has since rejoined his infantry regiment in the UK.

ABOVE Corporal Kiran Ale was born in Hong Kong and spent the first nine years of his life there and in Brunei due to his father's posting within a Gurkha infantry battalion, before the family returned to Nepal. Kiran moved back to Hong Kong after college and started working in construction. He tried out for the British Army and was selected in 2000, joining the Queen's Gurkha Signals and started working, among other postings, as a satellite communications operator in Iraq. Having returned to the UK, he was involved in a car accident which left him with severe facial injuries and killed one of his friends. Following a lengthy recovery, Kiran was deployed to Malta and then Libya, a member of the first ten-man team to mentor the transitional government in Benghazi, working while constantly surrounded by gunfire and the daily threat of suicide bombers. After a deployment to Somalia, again as part of a mentoring team, he was posted to Gurkha Company Sittang. He started to study Information Communication Technology at an open university in his free time and received his degree in 2008.

QUEEN'S GURKHA ENGINEERS

The QGE's role covers an extremely broad scope of field engineering and artisan trade duties in addition to their basic combat engineering skills, from bricklaying, building and structural finishing to carpentry and design draughtsmanship. They are electricians, welders, fitters, heating and plumbing technicians, plant vehicle operators and surveyors as well as combat divers. Many of them are also commando or parachute trained.

Engineers are usually some of the first units to be sent into combat zones alongside infantry troops in order to build camps and create infrastructure, with minimal protection, in mostly hostile environments. A number of men from the QGE have also been deployed as high-risk search units on operations, sent ahead of patrols in order to find and clear IEDs in support of bomb disposal experts.

The two squadrons of the QGE are currently based in Maidstone, Kent, and are integrated with the Corps of Royal Engineers. Small units of engineers from the QGE are frequently attached to other regiments as well, both in war and peacetime.

PREVIOUS PAGE Gurkha engineers frequently have to build structures during the night in preparation for infantry troops moving in at first light.

ABOVE WO2 Govinda Rana was born in west Nepal in a village without any electricity or proper roads but had a very happy childhood in Hong Kong, where his father, a Gurkha with the 2/2 GR, was posted. Govinda wanted to become a doctor, but when his father retired and began suffering from depression, Govinda, disillusioned with his job prospects in Nepal, decided to try to join the British Army, against his wife's as well as his parents' wishes. He was recruited to the QGE in 1994, then served in Kosovo as a tripwire and landmine spotter, and did one tour in Iraq and four in Afghanistan. On one deployment, he worked as a bomb disposal specialist, tasked with terrifying IED searches in pitch darkness, using night vision equipment and a metal detector. Whenever the army gave him time off, Govinda returned to Nepal to see his family and to take care of his father, whose illness deteriorated severely for a while and occupied Govinda's every waking moment. He is a certified mountaineer and rock-climbing leader and has completed several endurance races for charity.

WO2 Krishna Pun, a fitter mechanic by trade, has been serving in the QGE since 1995. The day he started his mandatory driver training as a young recruit was the first time he ever saw a car, let alone sat in one. During basic engineering training, he stripped engines in his spare time in order to understand how they worked. He served in Kosovo and twice in Iraq, building guard sangars (fortified troop positions) and field hospitals under the cover of night and erecting camps for up to 40,000 soldiers. Krishna also served two tours in Afghanistan, working as part of a search unit, identifying and defusing explosives, thereby saving innumerable lives. One of the most difficult memories from Krishna's service career is losing two close friends and subsequently having to recover their remains.

ABOVE WO2 Khadka Gurung's recruitment into the British Army seemed inevitable. His great-great-grandfather received the Indian Order of Merit in the First World War and his father, two brothers and several uncles and cousins were all soldiers. Khadka was very close to his parents, particularly his father. They encouraged him to pursue a university education and Khadka did begin a degree in biology, while also working as a teacher, but eventually he too joined the Gurkhas and was posted to the QGE in 1994. He was the first Gurkha ever to complete the arduous All Arms Commando Course, setting a precedent for several Gurkhas who have passed it since. He served in Kosovo alongside his brother clearing vast minefields, did two tours in Iraq, tasked, among other things, with restoring entire irrigation systems for the local population in the middle of a tribal war. Khadka also served in Afghanistan three times on very challenging operations, fighting close-quarter battles and constantly being surrounded by death. He got up every morning not expecting to live out the day. One of his most difficult memories from Afghanistan is of a medical evacuation his team was assigned to do, only to find upon their arrival that all the soldiers of the unit they had been sent to assist were either dead or severely injured after an enemy attack. Khadka's unit had to run in and out of the kill zone, extracting the remains of numerous colleagues.

RIGHT Sappers of the QGE building a bridge in very adverse weather conditions.

Demolition is as much a part of an engineer's skill set as construction.

During exercises, the QGE always rehearse infantry manoeuvres, such as casualty evacuation as well as attacking and defending positions, alongside their own specific technical training programme.

LEFT Corporal Jayandra Garbuja grew up near Pokhara, surrounded by soldiers – a number of his friends had joined the army, as had three brothers-in-law. He decided to apply as well and was selected for the QGE. Jayandra served in Iraq as a gunner and in Afghanistan building camp accommodation for arriving infantry soldiers. He chiefly remembers seeing enemy as well as friendly forces fall on a regular basis and struggling to come to terms with it. Upon his return, he completed the Commando Course and managed to become the top student out of 162 candidates. Becoming a Gurkha changed Jayandra's life completely, transforming him from a borderline-criminal teenager to a diligent, responsible soldier. He tries to make up for his dark early years by frequently making donations to charity. After two years training new recruits as a section commander in Catterick, he has now rejoined his regiment.

ABOVE Sapper Bijay Rana Magar comes from a long line of Gurkhas, but as there were not enough priests in his family, the boys were encouraged to become monks. Bijay moved to a Buddhist temple at the age of twelve in order to become a priest. He was required to cease all contact with his family and described that time as extremely difficult, but also credits it with turning him into a responsible person. The distance was hard for his family as well, so eventually they decided a normal education would be more beneficial: Bijay was returned home, finished school with distinction and started a BSc in biology. But when he saw a group of friends training for the British Army selection, he decided to give it a try as well. He was accepted and joined the QGE in 2009. Scoring top marks everywhere, he trained as an electrician and explosives search operator and deployed to Afghanistan in 2012 as part of an IED search unit. He is currently posted with his regiment in Kent, UK.

ABOVE When Corporal Lilaram Rai was twelve, his father, a doctor, was unjustly accused of a violent crime. It took ten years and all of the family's money and resources to exonerate him. Lila trained and worked as a medic at a hospital to contribute funds to the family's efforts, before joining the British Army in 2003. After basic training, he completed his basic engineering and trade courses with the QGE and became a drill instructor and PTI. He served two tours in Afghanistan, building forward operating bases and sangars under fire and training several teams in the search for explosives. After serving as one of the PTIs tasked with overseeing the physical tests at regional recruit selection in Nepal, Lila's current post is at the Infantry Training Centre in Yorkshire as a section commander, a position he has been aspiring to since his own basic training.

RIGHT Members of the QGE during an extended exercise on Salisbury Plain, UK.

LEFT AND ABOVE Construction or plant vehicles are driven by a group of engineers called 'planties'. These soldiers practise their speed, dexterity and expertise constantly, as on deployment they have to dig trenches and prepare vast areas for construction in record time.

QUEEN'S GURKHA SIGNALS

The QG Signals is a part of the Royal Corps of Signals and the four existing squadrons are stationed in four locations around the UK – Bramcote, Blandford, York and Stafford.

Gurkhas of the QG Signals regiment are trained in setting up, operating and repairing radio and data communications systems from simple wire transmitters to complex, state-of-the-art tactical fibre optics equipment. Their tasks in combat zones range from intercepting and disabling an enemy's communications to providing short- and long-distance links between different units and back to operations rooms and regimental headquarters. They build communications nets across vast geographical areas and are often the only lifeline that combat troops have in the field for requesting reinforcements or a medical evacuation. They have gained an excellent reputation within the British Military as well as internationally for their technical expertise.

The QG Signals has frequently been attached to international forces on NATO and UN deployments in addition to British military operations and a number of units are on standby to react to any sudden crisis immediately, with only hours to move out.

RIGHT A soldier from the QG Signals adjusts a communications mast.

PREVIOUS PAGES Signallers at an early stage of setting up a communications base.

LEFT Reception and data have to be constantly verified and adjusted once the established link is live. In combat, signals units sometimes intercept and block enemy transmissions.

ABOVE The most advantageous spot for setting up a good signals base is often in a very inhospitable location, mostly at the highest point of a geographical area, completely exposed to the elements. Occasionally, signals units have to hold these positions for long periods of time, taking turns to sleep in their communications vehicle so that their equipment is monitored continuously.

LEFT Major Dhan Bahadur Gurung grew up in a village headed by his grandfather and father, whom he credits with enabling him to have an excellent education, despite a less than secure financial standing. There were several Second World War veterans in the neighbourhood who often talked about their army lives. This got Dhan interested. He joined the Gurkhas in Hong Kong in 1980, initially as a clerk, but he eventually switched to the Queen's Gurkha Signals and trained as a radio technician. Dhan completed a tour in Kosovo, from which the haunting image of distraught old people and children squatting next to their burning houses is still a vivid memory. He later served the Royal Family as a Queen's Gurkha Orderly Officer, held several posts across and outside the Brigade and eventually was promoted to Officer in Command and subsequently Gurkha Major of his regiment. He holds an MBA from Plymouth University and has also regularly broken endurance race records such as that of the 100-km (62-mile) Trailwalker. His current post is 2nd in Command of the Blandford Garrison Support Unit.

ABOVE Captain Nim Pun of the Queen's Gurkha Signals comes from a military family but that wasn't the path he went down initially. He studied humanities, worked as a teacher and was very active in a student's union that was banned by the Nepalese government at the time. He didn't join the army and his regiment – then based in Hong Kong – until he was twenty. Under the old system, Gurkha soldiers weren't able to go home to Nepal to see their families for a long time after joining basic training and so Nim didn't see his daughter until she was three years old. He is a radio systems operator by trade, and is also a certified military parachutist. He has served in Hong Kong, Bosnia, Sierra Leone, Kosovo, Brunei and Afghanistan and then posted to the Infantry Training Centre in Catterick as a Platoon Commander, a job he enjoyed immensely. Nim has now moved to Brunei for his next posting.

Staff Sergeant Jagatram Rai grew up in a small village in the Everest region. His father was a teacher but his great-grandfather and two uncles were soldiers. Jagat gravitated towards literature and poetry at an early age and, even after being selected for the British Army in 2001 and joining the Queen's Gurkha Signals, he continued to write for magazines and radio, as well as publishing three books under the pen name Jagat Nabodit. He is also an accomplished poet and has won the National Poetry Award in Nepal. Jagat did a tour in Afghanistan as well as one in Italy, providing external communications for units serving in Libya, and is currently posted to a signals unit in Stafford, UK.

An equipment truck is manoeuvred into the right position during a QG Signals exercise in North Yorkshire.

LEFT Young signallers are frequently tested for speed and accuracy in setting up basic communications equipment.

ABOVE WO2 Tirthabahadur Rai joined the British Army in Hong Kong in 1992. His uncles were all Gurkhas and so was his grandfather, who died in a battle in Italy during the Second World War. Tir joined the Queen's Gurkha Signals, and a few years after his basic and trade training completed a military parachuting course. He served in Bosnia, did a tour in Kosovo, which he described as very difficult to process, and one in Afghanistan in 2008. He has held instructor posts across the Brigade, including one as a section commander with the Infantry Training Centre in Catterick, and was promoted to Sergeant Major in 2011. Tir has a knack for endurance races and has won the Trailwalker race a record six times.

Sig Hemraj Ghartimagar's father and several older relatives were all members of the Indian Army, and being a soldier was always Hemraj's dream. For a while though, it looked like fate would intervene, as both his parents died tragically when he was eight, an ordeal he found extremely difficult to cope with, particularly the death of his mother from cancer. He moved into an SOS Children's Village, an orphanage in Pokhara, with his younger brother and was cared for by a substitute parent – the orphanage typically grouped between nine and eleven children around one caretaker. But despite this difficult start in life, he never gave up his dream – he tried for and was accepted into the British Army in 2012 and joined the Queen's Gurkha Signals after completing basic training. As a Gurkha, Hemraj feels a huge amount of responsibility towards the British and wants to serve as an example for future Gurkhas. His older brother and sister-in-law also sadly died, and Hemraj tries, whenever he can, to care for his orphaned nephew who now lives at the same Pokhara orphanage.

Sig Pratap Rai is the first Gurkha in his extended family. Growing up with five sisters, he felt he needed to support them as well as his parents, so he tried for Gurkha selection, against his family's wishes, and was accepted in 2010, joining the Queen's Gurkha Signals after basic training. He has overcome a severe back injury, incurred in a training accident, is planning to study for an IT degree at the Open University and is currently posted to historic Blandford camp, a Dorset military base for many centuries. Pratap particularly enjoys engaging in conversations with the civilian public, especially elderly people, many of whom show a warm appreciation even towards very young Gurkhas.

QUEEN'S OWN GURKHA LOGISTIC REGIMENT

The members of the QOGLR have a wide range of expertise: they are drivers, logisticians and chefs. As drivers they operate large troop or equipment-carrying trucks, field tankers, tactical command vehicles as well as ambulances and passenger cars through any terrain and in all weather conditions. One of their most important tasks is to supply troops in combat zones or on exercises with equipment, ammunition, food rations and water.

In their logistics role, they acquire, record, store and distribute any kind of material or kit needed, act as load managers and provide maintenance and service of vehicles and infrastructure.

And in the Brigade of Gurkhas, where Nepalese traditions such as festive dress, food and music are a very important part of daily army life, the Gurkha chefs and their superior cooking skills are invaluable for raising morale. They frequently cook in the field, in harsh climates, under pressure, with very few ingredients, for hundreds of people at a time. With the British Army's recent cutbacks, the number of Gurkha chefs in particular has been significantly reduced. The ones that remain are irreplaceable assets of the Brigade.

Unlike the QGE and QG Signals, the QOGLR is a fully formed stand-alone unit with regimental headquarters and three squadrons, all based in Aldershot, UK. Various QOGLR personnel are also attached in support of other units within the British Army.

A QOGLR chef prepares dinner in a cooking tent containing several workstations and large portable freezing containers.

PREVIOUS PAGES A QOGLR driver moves equipment with a forklift truck.

ABOVE WO2 Deny Gurung comes from a family of Gurkhas, from both the Indian and British armies, and was always interested in becoming a soldier. He was recruited in 1993 and chose the logistics corps, defying his uncle who was Gurkha Major of an infantry battalion and wanted his nephew to follow in his footsteps. Deny served in Iraq, Bosnia, East Timor and Afghanistan, as well as with the Infantry Training Centre in the UK, and was promoted to Sergeant Major of his squadron in 2011. He is a Buddhist but describes his beliefs as a mix of the most enlightening theories from several religions. He was very close to his father, who died when Deny was twenty-one years old. Several years later, his father-in-law, the mayor of a town in west Nepal, was executed by militants. Deny's wife then returned to Nepal for a month to be with her grieving family, while Deny encountered life as a single parent for the first time – something he calls a bizarre but educational experience.

RIGHT Logisticians check stock at one of the regiment's large warehouses.

LEFT Sergeant Pritabahadur Gurung experienced no pressure at all to become a soldier, even though most of his relatives were Gurkhas. He joined the British Army in 1996 because he wanted to make a better life for himself and his family. He served in Bosnia as a driver and did two tours in Afghanistan as well as three in Iraq, back to back. The memories that keep coming back are of supply runs under heavy fire and his convoy being struck by an IED, resulting in a fatality. With his force protection unit, he rescued a number of men on an operation in Afghanistan and received the Queen's Commendation for Valuable Service award for his actions in combat. He is a keen runner and, in 1998, was part of the team winning the gruelling Trailwalker endurance race in nine hours and fifty-two minutes, a time still unbeaten to this day.

ABOVE Members of the QOGLR keep precise records of stored material and kit.

ABOVE Major Devendra Ale was born in Singapore, where his father, a soldier in the Gurkha Transport Regiment, was based. He grew up in both Hong Kong and Nepal, became a science major after graduating from secondary school and was also on the Nepalese national tae kwon do team when, against his father's wishes, he decided to try for the British Army in 1989. He joined as a clerk but later changed direction to become a military driver with the Gurkha Transport Regiment. Devendra served in Bosnia three times and was subsequently posted to Iraq to transport supplies – one of his main memories from that time is of the 400-km (250-mile) water resupply drives, through relentless sandstorms and with minimal protection. He also served in Afghanistan, as well as being one of only two Gurkhas per year selected to be a Queen's Gurkha Orderly Officer, splitting his time between his regular post and Buckingham Palace. Devendra is now his regiment's Gurkha Major.

RIGHT Major Kumar Gurung grew up in a military family with eight siblings. Two of his sisters passed away when he was a toddler, and a third died thirty years later. He still looks after her children, as well as the rest of his extended family. Kumar joined the Gurkhas in 1987 in Hong Kong, and was the champion recruit of his intake. He was selected for the Gurkha Transport Regiment, posted to Bosnia twice as part of a stabilising force and then deployed to Iraq. The latter was a tour he was certain he wouldn't come out of alive, comparing the experience to a horrible war movie. He was tasked with supplying and recovering troops under attack, through raging fires and acrid smoke, surrounded by dead bodies and livestock. It took Kumar five years to process that experience. After various posts to British Gurkhas Nepal, Brunei and a tense UN mission in Cyprus, he served in Afghanistan and as a Queen's Gurkha Orderly Officer. Kumar is a hobby architect and designed and built his own house. He has recently taken over as Officer in Command of a unit in the British Army tasked with training and administrative support.

LEFT Cooking dinner during an exercise in Kenya. Gurkha chefs do their best to prepare popular traditional Nepalese dishes even in the most remote locations.

ABOVE Corporal Yam Sunuwar was married by the age of seventeen. He reluctantly left his pregnant wife to go through the lengthy Gurkha recruitment process, even though being a soldier was all he wanted to be, having grown up with his father's stories of army life. He had just passed selection when he received word that his wife had gone into labour, so his commanders let him leave for a few hours to visit her and his new baby daughter in the hospital. Yam joined the Gurkha Transport Regiment in 1996 and served in Kosovo and Bosnia, training drivers from various different countries and leading supply convoys to and from battlegroups. He was also posted to Iraq, a harrowing deployment, and served two tours in Afghanistan, tasked with load management on the first and military intelligence on the second. He is currently posted to the Gurkha Welfare Office in Aldershot, a job he volunteered for, assisting military veterans with their day-to-day lives and works part time for an IT company, doing game design and management.

ROYAL GURKHA RIFLES

The first Gurkhas ever to be recruited into the British Army were infantry soldiers. Unlike all other regiments in the British Army, every soldier from every specialist or corps regiment in the Brigade of Gurkhas, from engineers to band members, are trained as infantry first and only then do they receive their specialist training.

Today's Brigade of Gurkhas has one infantry regiment, the Royal Gurkha Rifles, split into two battalions, 1 RGR and 2 RGR. One is based in Brunei, the other in the UK, and they rotate every three to four years. They are commanded by a number of Gurkha officers who have been promoted through the ranks as well as British officers trained at the Royal Military Academy Sandhurst.

The RGR was formed by amalgamating the four old Gurkha infantry regiments (2 GR, 6 GR, 7 GR and 10 GR) in the mid-1990s, when the Brigade base in Hong Kong was closed down. Historically, 1 RGR was made up of individuals from west Nepal and eastern Nepalese recruits went to 2 RGR. This has changed in the past few years and now an equal balance of soldiers from east and west is maintained in both battalions.

RIGHT An RGR soldier gets ready for a vehicle patrol in Afghanistan.

PREVIOUS PAGES RGR soldiers of the Fire Support Group (FSG) provide top cover for troops practising an attack on lower ground.

ABOVE Each company of the RGR is named after a famous battle, for example, Gallipoli (Turkey, First World War) or Tamandu (Burma, Second World War). These battle honours, awarded to military units for their achievements in certain campaigns, are celebrated with parades on designated days of the year.

RIGHT RGR soldiers during a river crossing in Brunei, a country that permanently hosts one of the two RGR battalions at any given time.

Corporal Chandra Suba Gurung joined the Gurkha infantry in 2001. He was already playing competitive football by the age of five – it is a sport he has never given up, winning the Brigade-based Nepal Cup football tournament with his team right after joining the British Army. Chandra served in Bosnia twice and has a few rare but happy memories of football matches with soldiers from other countries during those deployments. He also participated in a rescue operation in Ivory Coast and completed three tours in Afghanistan. It was there that he experienced being shot at and firing his rifle in return for the first time. He remembers the daily shock of seeing people die – colleagues, allies, enemy fighters, civilians and even children. He once shared a cigarette with a friend who only minutes later was caught in the blast radius of a suicide bomber and killed instantly, walking just 20 metres behind him. Despite such experiences, Chandra still felt a sense of achievement teaching valuable skills to local forces and forging friendships with Afghan soldiers and civilians. He was posted to Gurkha Company Catterick as a section commander in 2013.

Corporal Yam Roka Pun joined the RGR in 2004 and was posted to Musa Qala, Helmand Province, within a year, the first of three deployments to Afghanistan. Facing life in a warzone, he reverted back to his childhood passion of writing poetry, which helped him express his experiences of enduring daily enemy attacks and losing colleagues but also finding a brotherhood that is forged among soldiers in battle. Yam has now left the Gurkhas but has been posted to Afghanistan again, as part of a logistics regiment of the British Army. He still continues to write when he can. One of the poems that he wrote while on nightly guard duty in a lonely fortified sangar, was published a number of times:

> This is the place where rocks melt into sand / And the bitch wind blows it into your face
> For minutes visibility is zero / For days you eat dust / And for months dust will eat you.
> I stay in a lonely tower / Neither birds sing nor rains shower
> There goes another twister again / Round and round with desert sand
> As even Hell freezes over in this no man's land.
> Ups and downs with so many bends / Dusty roads that never end
> And empty sky that reflects virgin lands
> So many pains with no gain / But still the war remains.
> In the city, silent nights leave only watchful eyes awake,
> And I stay here as they sit only metres ahead
> Evil roars as the war begins / Peace is dead or whatever that means
> What dreadful atrocity, all my awakening dreams.

LEFT A Gurkha of the RGR operates a javelin anti-tank weapon during an exercise in northern Australia.

ABOVE Captain Ram Rai always wanted to be a Gurkha. When he was nineteen, the Galla Wallahs came to his village and recruited him into the British Army. He served in Bosnia and afterwards in East Timor, a very difficult tour. Ram had to lead a reconnaissance team into a battle in which they were heavily outnumbered. They still managed to prevail. His unit also rescued and evacuated a large number of people being held hostage in the jungle by local militias. He remembers the appallingly squalid living conditions of the local population that his regiment was sent in to help. Ram also served two tours in Sierra Leone and three in Afghanistan, and has several memories that are still very much present in his mind – watching a colleague die after desperately performing CPR on him for several minutes and dragging a fatally wounded member of his unit away from an IED blast site. Ram is a certified paratrooper, an expert tracker and a much sought-after jungle warfare instructor. One of his peers once said that Ram would always put himself in harm's way if there was a chance he could save a life.

ABOVE Sergeant Govinda Gurung had a happy childhood growing up in an army family in west Nepal. He always wanted to be a soldier and joined the RGR in 2002. He served twice in Bosnia, once in Kosovo and twice in Afghanistan. On one of the Afghanistan tours, a helicopter crashed into the sangar he was guarding and Govinda was buried in rubble and debris. He managed to free himself and started digging frantically for a colleague who was buried with him, but only managed to pull out his dead body. On the second Afghanistan tour, Govinda's patrol base was attacked. There were two fatalities, among them his commanding officer and, as his immediate superior was on leave, Govinda took charge of the situation and the troops involved, a responsibility that went above and beyond his rank at the time. His actions earned him a Mention in Dispatches, a citation for bravery in combat – a high military honour. Govinda is now posted to Catterick as a platoon sergeant. He tries to remember his fallen comrades every day.

RIGHT Larger weapons like general purpose machine guns (GPMGs) or anti-tank weaponry are usually transported by individual soldiers on foot.

LEFT AND ABOVE Infantry soldiers of the RGR perform frequent night-time exercises, with and without night-vision equipment.

ABOVE Colour Sergeant Arunhang Nembang joined the RGR in 1999, a spontaneous change of heart, as he was originally set to study law. Arun served in Sierra Leone and as a sniper in Iraq. In between operational deployments abroad, he worked alongside the Gallas during Gurkha selection in Nepal, a posting he very much enjoyed. During three tours in Afghanistan, he earned a stellar record and the respect of his peers as well as commanding officers. Arun doesn't like to talk much about his achievements, but his former colleagues and commanders remember several courageous acts, such as the time Arun intercepted an enemy ambush in Afghanistan, saving a number of lives. He is currently posted in Kent, with his regiment.

RIGHT Colour Sergeant Basanta Rai grew up in an army family, often playing soldier and was even taken to the jungle for a bit of training by his father, the highly respected Gurkha Major of the 10 GR infantry battalion. Basanta is the only one of his brothers who really wanted to become a soldier and he joined the RGR in 1999. His career has mostly consisted of postings in reconnaissance units: one deployment to Bosnia, one to Sierra Leone and four to Afghanistan, where he was also a member of a police mentoring unit and was hugely popular with his colleagues as well as the Afghan police officers he trained with patience and respect. His brave actions in Afghanistan – covering a troop retreat and pulling injured soldiers out of a kill zone under fire – earned him a Mention in Dispatches.

EXERCISES AND OPERATIONS

Operational deployments are what Gurkhas are trained for. They can last from just a few weeks to several months and require a broad spectrum of skills, all of which are honed during exercises at home and abroad. Overseas exercises in particular test strategy, teamwork and leadership of troops and officers alike by reproducing wartime situations and environments, complete with live fire and enemies, who are usually played by colleagues.

PREVIOUS PAGE A police mentor from the RGR introduces a new Afghan National Police recruit to the basics of rifle assembly and use.

ABOVE AND RIGHT Large military vehicles on operations use what is known as a top-cover: a soldier in a turret scans the horizon for potential dangers and defends the vehicle against attackers, using a heavy machine gun.

LEFT AND ABOVE RGR soldiers frequently rehearse different attack approaches – with small troop sections, larger platoons or entire companies – through fire and smoke, exposed to extreme temperatures in countries such as Kenya and Australia.

FOLLOWING PAGES Soldiers are transported to an attack location by a Blackhawk helicopter of the Australian Defence Force during an exercise.

LEFT AND ABOVE All Gurkha regiments regularly practise khukri and rifle drills. Infantry battalions have additional units that specialise in short-range weapons like mortars.

ABOVE Lance Corporal Niranjan Gurung got into a lot of fights growing up. He moved to India to go to college, primarily to change the direction in which his life was heading. He studied commerce for a year before returning to Nepal to join the British Army in 2004. He was selected for the QGE, trained as a plant operator and military diver, certified as a PTI and eventually also took up boxing and training for Iron Man competitions, which he won in 2009 and 2010. Niranjan was deployed to Afghanistan in 2008 and remembers driving a huge construction vehicle in a convoy for thirteen days and nights, crossing rivers and bridges, constantly exposed to mortar and small arms fire as well as IEDs. For soldiers at war, getting shot at becomes strangely routine – a fact that Niranjan was surprised to discover. He survived several near-misses: on one occasion, two plant vehicles drove over the same spot and one of them – his – just missed the IED that exploded under the vehicle directly following him. Niranjan served as a PTI during the 2013 regional Gurkha selection and is now posted to the Infantry Training Centre in Catterick.

RIGHT Corporal Kamal Thapa Magar grew up in a village in Gorkha, 10 km (6 miles) from the nearest school – a distance he walked every day for several years. He started serious weightlifting when he was a teenager and was runner-up in the Mr. Pokhara bodybuilding competition in 2001. This proved to be an unlikely disadvantage the first time he tried out for the British Army, as he had too much bulk for the tasks he was required to perform. He returned the next year and was accepted, joining the QOGLR in 2002 and soon after was posted to Iraq, where he was on supply-run duty. He was serving in Afghanistan in 2009 as part of a reconnaissance unit attached to Special Forces that ended up in an area surrounded and fired upon by the enemy. Kamal was shot in the right shoulder, but still managed to manoeuvre his vehicle around so his unit could return fire, and to subsequently extract them from the kill zone driving with only one arm and bleeding profusely. He is still incredibly grateful to the medic, who kept him awake and talking for forty minutes during his evacuation and who tragically died in an IED blast shortly afterwards. Kamal served as the personal driver to the Colonel of the Brigade of Gurkhas before rejoining his regiment in Aldershot.

LEFT AND ABOVE Gurkhas are specially trained to camouflage themselves effectively in jungle and grassy environments, a skill that is sharpened practically from the first day of service.

FOLLOWING PAGES In the later stages of the Afghanistan campaign, Gurkhas were mainly deployed in mentoring roles for the local police and armed forces. As they showed an enormous amount of respect for the culture of their charges and shared a common language (many Nepalis and Afghans speak Urdu), the Gurkhas became very popular teachers.

LEFT Major Prembahadur Ale was born in Hong Kong. Interested in doing a medical degree, he began studying science in college before his Gurkha father convinced him to try out for the British Army. Prem did so, not wanting to disappoint his parents, and was recruited and selected for the Queen's Gurkha Signals in 1986. He is a systems telecommunications engineer by trade and has held various instructional posts over the years. However, he has also always been deeply immersed in literature and science, and has continuously pursued a broad, high-level education throughout his army career, achieving a Bachelor's degree with honours in politics and international relations as well as a Master's with distinction in international security. He is currently in the initial stages of a PhD in Southern Asian national security issues. Prem values a good work-life balance and devotes his spare time to his family, gardening and his eight chickens.

ABOVE Corporal Joseph Subba's father and two uncles were Gurkhas. He received his education at an English boarding school and was a self-described bully as a teenager. Joseph concedes that the army as well as religion, now a big factor in his life, changed him completely. He was selected for the QGE in 2004, completing his engineering courses as well as PTI training and the Commando Course, and subsequently did two tours in Afghanistan. He was part of a unit doing night-time construction of accommodation camps in pitch darkness while constantly being covered in sand, only to switch to daytime camp construction after a few weeks, in 50°C (122°F) heat, wearing full body armour, while being fired upon regularly. After the unit suffered a fatality, Joseph started using intense physical exercise to come to terms with the incident. He is currently one of the dedicated section commanders at the Infantry Training Centre.

ABOVE AND RIGHT RGR soldiers on exercise near Townsville, northern Australia.

LEFT AND ABOVE The Gurkhas have a reputation for being highly skilled jungle fighters. Most of them feel at home in a jungle environment like Brunei and several are expert trackers, often tasked with teaching jungle warfare skills to other allied forces.

ABOVE Captain Kamal Khapung Limbu grew up in India and Nepal. His family was headed by a veteran Gurkha Major from the 10 GR who was persecuted and exiled to India for leading a national political referendum. After completing secondary school, Kamal studied in the mornings and taught at a boarding school in the afternoons to finance a BA in commerce before joining the Queen's Gurkha Engineers in Hong Kong in 1991. He served in South Korea as part of an Honour Guard before postings to Bosnia and Cyprus. He then completed two tours in Afghanistan and two in Iraq as part of engineering units tasked with reconnaissance patrols and the clearing of IEDs as well as with building camps, bridges, dams, roads and schools, seeing heavy combat along the way. He was the first Gurkha to ever head the Royal Engineers Troop Commander's course, has an MBA from Northampton University and is now the Training Officer at the Infantry Training Centre in Catterick.

RIGHT Rifleman Surya Jirel grew up with extremely varied interests. When he was a child, he discovered a passion for painting, which his parents encouraged by sending him to stay with an artist in order to learn the basic techniques when he was twelve. As he grew older, Surya then wanted to go into biotechnology or the medical field, but eventually he decided to follow in his great-grandfather's footsteps and joined the RGR in 2011. He was one of the fittest soldiers among his peers and made it on to the army championship volleyball team, playing matches in Holland and Germany. Surya served in Afghanistan, taking part in counter-insurgency operations and working in alliance with Afghan armed forces, but through it all, he has always kept his paints and brushes with him. His stunning paintings of patrolling soldiers have garnered high praise. Surya is currently stationed in Brunei with his regiment.

PREVIOUS PAGES Troops are transported back to their base after an exercise that mimicked an Afghan combat environment.

ABOVE Sergeant Naresh Gurung grew up in Bhojpur, east Nepal, with two brothers and his parents, who were both teachers. Despite being the middle child and thus not tasked with being the main carer for his parents according to Nepalese tradition, he has always felt a certain responsibility for them as well as his brothers, and has been supporting them on every level since he was accepted into the British Army. Naresh joined the RGR in 2001 and found that the hardest thing to deal with was not seeing his wife for four whole years due to continuous courses and deployments. Their only contact was during rare phone calls that his wife was able to accept at the local greengrocer's shop phone. Naresh served in Bosnia and Sierra Leone and was posted to Afghanistan four times. Despite being very outspoken, he has a remarkable military track record – a former commander once described him as the best of the best.

Corporal Chandra Dev Rai's father served in the Indian Army for twenty-two years. There was quite a bit of pressure on Chandra to follow in his father's footsteps, but he chose the British Army instead and joined the RGR in 1996. He served in East Timor, a frightening first deployment that made him think frequently about feeling too young to die and the possibility of not seeing his family again. He was also deployed to Bosnia and to Afghanistan four times, as an instructor to the Afghan National Army and as part of the peacekeeping force in Helmand, living through countless attacks and suffering the heartbreaking loss of colleagues. His latest post is as an instructor to new recruits at the Infantry Training Centre in Catterick. Chandra sees his job as a soldier partly as an opportunity to help people in need, while observing and respecting their cultures and religions.

LEFT AND ABOVE Soldiers preparing food and relaxing at a patrol base in Afghanistan. Close ties were established with surrounding goat farmers and market stall holders, so that the occasional freshly cooked meal was guaranteed.

ABOVE Rifleman Sunil Limbu had always wanted to join the Gurkhas, like his grandfathers and uncle before him. He joined the RGR in 2009 and served in Afghanistan twice. On one of those deployments, he was at a patrol base that was attacked by the enemy and was thrown to the ground by a mortar explosion. Despite incurring numerous fragment injuries on both arms and legs, he ran to his colleagues, who were wounded and lying on open ground, and dragged them to safety. He had nightmares about it for weeks afterwards, but eventually they stopped. What remained from the incident is some shrapnel in his legs as well as a Military Cross he was awarded for his bravery.

RIGHT Gurkhas posted to Helmand Province, Afghanistan, enjoy a friendly evening volleyball game. The Gurkhas are formidable adversaries not just in battle, but also in sports.

LEFT Gurkha soldiers practise abseiling in full kit from a Bell UH-1 'Huey' helicopter, in Brunei.

ABOVE Corporal Chaman Balal was raised by his beloved mother and grandmother, as his father, a Gurkha with the Indian Army, was largely absent. He played semi-professional volleyball and worked as a farmer for a while before deciding on an army career himself. Chaman served in Sierra Leone, where he was in a serious vehicle accident and spent six months in hospital, having lost part of his memory. The accident changed his outlook on life and made him more accepting and balanced. After his recovery, he deployed to Ivory Coast on a rescue mission and on three tours to Afghanistan, experiencing all the terrors a warzone can throw at a soldier. Chaman processes his thoughts and experiences by writing them down in several carefully and beautifully kept old notebooks, a habit he started when he was a teenager. His last post was as a section commander at the Infantry Training Centre, a job very dear to his heart. He has now returned to his regiment in Brunei.

LEFT There are no Gurkhas in Corporal Surya Hanggam's extended family – his father is a prominent politician in Nepal. His mother left the family when Surya was only twelve, and he didn't cope well with the loss of a parent, quickly starting to slide down the wrong track in life. At some point, however, he decided to leave his troubled past behind, first turning to Christianity and then joining the army in 2000. Surya is a trained medic and PTI, and he served in Bosnia once and in Afghanistan twice. He left the army halfway through his career, after his brother, a politician like his father, was ambushed and murdered, causing him to rethink his life and take a break. Eventually he decided to return and was posted to Catterick as a PTI. Surya's dream for his life, post-retirement, is to build and run an orphanage in Nepal.

ABOVE Colour Sergeant Jiwan 'J.P.' Gurung was inspired to try out for the British Army by his father and uncle, both Gurkhas. He was selected on his first try in 1998 and came top in every course during his career, right from the beginning. J.P. served in Kosovo, Bosnia and Afghanistan and became one of only a handful of Gurkhas to be selected for a special operations unit, a posting he held for six years. He also completed three tours and countless deployments in Iraq, experiencing extreme situations , including jumping out of a plane at 5,500 metres (18,000 feet) in the middle of the night during a counter-insurgency mission, and surviving a helicopter crash that killed two of his colleagues, a memory that refuses to fade. J.P. returned to his regiment as one of the youngest Gurkhas ever to be promoted to Sergeant. He was 26. He has since become the first Gurkha in history to be posted to the Royal Military Academy at Sandhurst as an officer cadet instructor.

FOLLOWING PAGES The end of a long exercise at a remote outpost in Kenya.

ABOVE Corporal Hangdip Rai was born into a family with an illustrious history in the
Gurkhas. He joined the RGR in 2000, having grown up mesmerised by the war stories told
by his grandfather, a Second World War veteran. After a deployment to Bosnia and one to
Afghanistan, Hangdip was designated as a medic and started his training, honing his skills
for four years before being deployed to Afghanistan again, this time as part of the Royal
Medical Corps. Being a medic in a warzone is a distressing task. He has had to perform first
aid on numerous victims of an IED explosion with barely any equipment and using vehicle
parts as stretchers – the medical kit had been destroyed by the blast. His deployments have
consisted of daily medical evacuations under sniper fire, pulling soldiers from burning cars,
trying to keep people with horrific blast injuries alive long enough to fly them to safety – a
constant effort to save lives. When he retires from the army, Hangdip wants to become either
a paramedic or firefighter.

RIGHT Corporal Prithvi Rai's family included several Gurkhas. His grandfather, father, uncles
and cousin were all soldiers. Prithvi had a bit of an itinerant childhood for that reason,
growing up mostly in Hong Kong and India. He practised tae kwon do regularly and planned
on becoming a doctor. When he returned to Nepal, he adjusted quickly to his native
environment, which had become a little unfamiliar over the years. Having discarded a handful
of other plans, Prithvi decided to join the British Army. He served in Afghanistan twice where
he experienced the trauma of losing friends in combat and having to go to work every day
not knowing whether he would come back alive. In his spare time, he plans and invests in
infrastructure projects in Nepal.

LEFT Lance Corporal Seemoon Limbu joined the Gurkhas in 2008 and was immediately off to a flying start. He was champion recruit of his intake and straight after joining the RGR, he was posted to south Afghanistan as part of a mechanised infantry unit. He deployed there once more, three years later. He came in first in the JLC, the most important first exam in a young Gurkha's career, receiving an instant promotion to Lance Corporal. Seemoon feels that being a Gurkha carries an enormous responsibility and is very aware that his words and actions on and off duty reflect on the entire Brigade as well as thousands of ancestors. He was once described as an extremely bright hope for the future of the Brigade of Gurkhas.

ABOVE Sergeant Jitendra Rai grew up in a family full of teachers and enjoyed a very good education. He was the top student throughout his years at school and went to college after graduation, but had always harboured a desire to join either the police or the armed forces. He ended up trying for the British Army and was selected in 1998. Jitendra was part of the first British Army unit to deploy to Sierra Leone and went on to serve in Bosnia. He was also posted to Afghanistan twice – tours he doesn't like to remember. He is a certified jungle warfare instructor and is called 'The Human GPS' by his colleagues for his uncanny ability, they say, to 'find his way out of the deepest, darkest hole'. He is currently posted to Catterick as a platoon sergeant.

On overseas exercises, local towns and villages are sometimes involved in the action, providing personnel and property. In return, the Gurkhas help them with infrastructure and basic needs.

An infantry unit forms a troop convoy, making strategic use of top cover.

A Gurkha soldier taking a moment of rest on top of a trench during an exercise in Kenya.

When Lance Corporal Topjang Rai was a child, he already showed a keen interest in engineering, taking things apart to see how they worked. When he was fourteen, his family fled their quiet village in Solukhumbu, east Nepal, to escape armed militants threatening the region, and they settled in Kathmandu. His father is a boarding school principal, so education was a big priority in his family. Topjang was recruited into the British Army in 2009 and was selected for the QGE, his obvious first choice of regiment. He believes in research, education and asking many questions, and he is trained in operating plant vehicles as well as searching and dismantling explosives. He was also the only junior rank to get a Commando Course certificate, coming first in his class. Topjang aims to become a section commander in Catterick.

ABOVE Corporal Raju Tamang's brother died when he was four years old. He doesn't remember what his brother looked like and no one in his family had a camera, as they were not common in his village, so there are no photographs to remember him by. Raju takes plenty of pictures of his own children now. Growing up, he often saw a number of relatives and his grandfather come and go, wearing uniform. He thought they looked smart, so he wanted to try for the army as well. He was accepted in the RGR in 1998, served in Kosovo and then twice in Bosnia. There, he was part of a unit searching civilian houses for weapons, and developed a deep sympathy for the people having their homes turned upside down by soldiers. He then deployed to Afghanistan as part of an IED search unit and as top gunner of large military vehicles. It was the first time he ever had to fire a weapon at a human being. Having experienced the loss of colleagues and friends, he developed an accepting attitude towards life and death. Raju is a PTI and currently serves in Catterick, which has been one of his dreams since he was in basic training.

RIGHT Corporal Kedar Singjali didn't enjoy school much, so he joined the British Army in order to support his family. He had always been an exceptional runner and broke several records during basic training. Being a chef was not his first choice but he was selected for the Gurkha Transport Regiment in 1997, started cookery training immediately afterwards and soon came to love it. He served in Kosovo twice, in Iraq once and completed three tours in Afghanistan. Kedar's memories from his tours are varied and colourful, ranging from being attacked by the enemy and the very unpleasant practice of having to burn camp waste for weeks on end to browsing bustling Afghan markets in order to buy fresh produce. While posted to Brunei, he started to carve sculptures out of food, now one of his signature skills. Kedar has won several cookery awards, two of them national. He has recently left the Gurkhas and transferred to the Royal Navy as a chef.

LEFT Corporal Sunil Gurung's father and grandfather were Gurkhas in the Indian Army and Sunil spent his childhood in India – a time and place he fondly remembers. There were no telephones where he grew up, so he lost contact with most of his childhood friends, which he regrets. He speaks seven Hindu dialects on top of Nepalese and English. Sunil joined the British Army in 2001, serving two tours in Bosnia, one in Sierra Leone and three in Afghanistan. He had a couple of near-misses while on operations – once when a grenade was thrown into a tent he had just vacated and another time when his patrol drove into the blast radius of an IED. He started working in Military Intelligence a few years after joining the Gurkhas and has been posted to intelligence cells across the British Army ever since.

ABOVE Gurkhas on morning patrol during a tactical exercise. The future of Gurkha service in the British Army is not entirely clear, but for now, the 2,500 remaining troops continue to build the legend of a brigade of knights that has fascinated the world for 200 years.

4

RETIREMENT

In the past, before Gurkhas had gained the right to settle in the UK and to equal pensions, retired soldiers would traditionally return to Nepal. Today, Gurkhas leaving the army have the option to remain in the UK. They are well educated as well as adapted to British culture and go on to work in a variety of professions. Some of them are academics, some run their own businesses and others find employment in areas as varied as security, hospitality, technology, management and social work. All of them, whatever their fate, are immensely proud to have served in the British Army and not a single one regrets their choice of becoming a Gurkha.

RETIRED GURKHAS fall into one of three categories. There are soldiers who are discharged due to illness or injury, who receive treatment and compensation but usually have quite a hard time adjusting to life outside the army – their careers were cut short and they are on average relatively young.

Others are soldiers at the end of their careers, having served the maximum time or been made redundant. They usually adjust well to life after the army, and go into reserve units, or work in security or civilian jobs. Some are academics, having completed an advanced education during their army career, while others set up their own businesses.

Finally, there are the veterans who retired before Gurkhas received the right to settle in the UK. These men generally went back to Nepal after their service, where many turned to farming. Some still reside at home, while a number of them live out their lives in retirement homes. The right to settle was granted in 2004 to those who retired after 1997, although most are keen to return home to Nepal as soon as their children have finished their education.

In 2009, that right was extended to all ex-Gurkhas, and since then, some of the elder veterans have moved to the UK.

The fate and treatment of retired Gurkha soldiers has also changed in other ways. In the 1960s and 70s, the Gurkhas received a pension of just a couple of pounds per month. This gradually increased over the years, and now, soldiers who retired in or after 1997 (the year the Brigade moved its headquarters from Hong Kong to the UK) receive retirement payments equal to their British and Commonwealth colleagues.

Currently, there are a number of elderly retired Gurkhas living in both Nepal and the UK. They are taken care of by the Gurkha Welfare Trust, a charity providing welfare pensions, financial and medical aid, education, hardship grants and community projects to Gurkha ex-servicemen and their dependants in all corners of Nepal. They also run two advice and support centres in the UK, which help relocated veterans with paperwork, language, pension matters and sometimes just moral and emotional support.

RIGHT Rifleman Gumansing Thapa joined the Gurkhas in 1947. Selected in India, he spent a year as a guide for other recruits and went on to participate in intense battles during the lengthy Malayan offensive (1948–1960). He is reluctant to go into the details of his combat history, which is still painful for him, but has an enduring memory of being permanently on the brink of starvation while lying in wait to ambush the enemy in the deep jungle. Gumansing left the army in 1952 and has since moved to the UK, where he helps other members of the Nepalese community with their day-to-day lives.

Rifleman Vinod Budhathoki joined the Gurkhas in 2005 and, after a tour in Bosnia, found his passion in jungle training while stationed in Brunei. In 2010 he deployed to Helmand Province in southern Afghanistan, where he was often put in first position during foot patrols to check for IEDs. One day he stepped on one, resulting in the loss of both legs and two fingers, as well as a severe head injury. Vinod remembers being conscious the entire time from the moment of his injury to his evacuation by helicopter. He was put in an artificial coma for two weeks and started physical rehabilitation immediately afterwards. He has adjusted well to his high-tech prosthetics and now lives a happy family life with his wife and two children. Vinod has not felt any regret for even a minute about joining the Gurkhas, and misses the army every day.

Corporal Agnish Thapa grew up in Gorkha. Most members of his family have served in the Indian Army, and Agnish joined the British Army in 2002. During an intense firefight in Afghanistan in 2007, surrounded by the enemy and low on ammunition, he left cover and dragged an injured Australian soldier out of the kill zone. He was awarded the Military Cross for his courageous and selfless actions. In 2010, again deployed to Afghanistan and again surrounded by the enemy, he was severely injured by an RPG round, which took off his left arm almost completely. After multiple surgeries and rehabilitation procedures to remove shrapnel from his body, he has regained the use of his arm but is no longer able to serve in the military. Agnish was once described by one of his commanding officers as the outstanding soldier of his generation.

ABOVE Lance Corporal Ram Basnet joined the British Army in 1979. He served in Hong Kong and the Falklands. At the time, the families of Gurkhas below the rank of corporal were not allowed to join them from Nepal, but once, for a three-year period during his service in Hong Kong, Ram was able to bring his family over to live with him. He described it as the happiest time of his life. He retired in 1992 and, with a couple of other ex-Gurkhas, opened a non-profit boarding school for 400–500 children. From 2001 to 2008, he worked as a security guard at a foreign embassy in Afghanistan in a job environment he likened to a prison – security employees are not allowed to leave their respective compounds and are subject to the dangers of rocket attacks and insurgent violence. Ram now works as a Galla, one of the retired Gurkhas serving at the annual selection, weighing, measuring and testing potential new recruits.

RIGHT WO2 Bishnu Tamang joined the Gurkhas in 1984 when their headquarters were still in Hong Kong. During basic training, he taught himself English by reading a dictionary every night in his bunk, by torchlight. He served on operations in Bosnia and Sierra Leone and retired from the British Army in 2004. Bishnu received his MBA in 2008 and now co-owns a very successful security company with more than 350 employees. He uses some of the proceeds from his business for his passion: supporting infrastructure projects and charities in Nepal.

Corporal Mani Lohorung Rai joined the RGR in 1991 and served for twenty-two years – most notably in Belize, Sierra Leone and Afghanistan as well as Catterick, where he was a section commander for new recruits. Upon retirement, he retrained to be a plumber and now runs his own plumbing and heating business in Kent. Mani found it as hard to readapt to life as a civilian as it had been to change from a civilian into a soldier. He eventually wants to return to Nepal to serve his country by doing charity work.

Corporal Khil Thapa joined the army in 1990 without telling his parents, completed basic training in Hong Kong and moved to the UK with the QGE in 1994. One of his strongest memories is of seeing a little girl climb out from a collapsed building in Bosnia, and not being able to do much to help. To this day he wonders what happened to her. Khil cleared landmines in Bosnia and served in both Kosovo and Iraq. When he felt it was time for him to see what else was out there, he quit the army, learned how to paraglide and spent a lot of time at Everest base camp, twice climbing almost all the way up to the summit, and it was then that he understood that the mountains were where he belonged. He now runs his own trekking company in Kathmandu and tries to go climbing whenever he can.

Major Biswanath Rai was recruited into the British Army in 1965. He walked for seven days and seven nights to get to the recruitment camp in east Nepal. From there, the successful recruits were taken to Calcutta and put on a ship to Malaysia, where central selection took place at the time. Biswanath had endured a very strict upbringing and regular beatings as a child so the intense basic training proved no problem for him. He was part of the border patrol in Hong Kong, and then worked as a medic and as a jungle warfare instructor in Belize. After a very fast series of promotions, he was appointed Gurkha Major of his regiment, the 10 GR. He retired in 1994, now resides in Kathmandu, and is an avid golfer.

Captain Trilochan Gurung's career in the Gurkhas started in 1987 and saw him serve in Hong Kong, Bosnia and Sierra Leone, as well as completing two tours in Afghanistan. He led a unit on a difficult operation in the Sangin district of Afghanistan, in the middle of the night, to extract friendly forces from a kill zone, who had suffered two fatalities during an insurgent attack. The ensuing brutal firefight lasted for three hours and was conducted almost entirely in pitch darkness. A total of thirty-six soldiers were saved that night and Trilochan was awarded a Mention in Dispatches. He also served as one of two Queen's Gurkha Orderly Officers, chosen annually from among decorated high-ranking Gurkhas. He is a member of the Royal Victorian Order and now works as a senior consultant at a luxury chauffeur service in the UK.

Captain Ganesh Kumar Rai joined the Gurkhas in 1982 in Hong Kong. Almost all the men in his family were Gurkhas. He served in Belize, Bosnia, Sierra Leone, Kosovo and Afghanistan and, from those experiences, he mostly remembers the squalor that the conflicts created for the people living there – the homelessness in a completely destroyed Sarajevo and the starvation in Sierra Leone. After retiring in 2008, he worked as a security operations manager for the 2012 London Olympics and then, like his father before him, accepted a posting as a recruitment officer for the annual Gurkha selection in Nepal.

Colour Sergeant Tekbahadur Mabo grew up during the 1970s in east Nepal. His family was suddenly plunged into poverty when his younger brother became severely ill and all the family's money was needed for his treatment. Tek started working as a primary school teacher to support his parents before joining the Gurkhas in 1991. He has spent a large part of his career in the RGR on operations, serving in Bosnia, Sierra Leone, Macedonia and four tours in Afghanistan. He was described by one of his former commanding officers as a world-class soldier, particularly in the field of anti-tank warfare. Tek retired in 2013 and is now working in security management in the UK.

LEFT Captain Lachyabahadur 'L.B.' Gurung had an illustrious twenty-six-year career in the Brigade of Gurkhas. He served in Belize, Afghanistan and on several difficult operations in Bosnia and Kosovo, trying to defuse ethnic tensions and searching for IEDs. One of these devices killed two of his colleagues, whose bodies he had to recover. L.B. also served as a training officer in Catterick and as a recruitment officer for Gurkha selection in Nepal. Immediately after retirement, he went to Iraq as a security project manager for FSI Worldwide, an ex-Gurkha recruitment company. He is now an operations manager there and lives and works in Dubai.

ABOVE Captain Gajendra Dewan met Gurkha soldiers for the first time when he was fifteen years old. They spoke of their lives in the army and their daring adventures and Gajendra was hooked. He joined the British Army in 1987 and was selected for the 10 GR. Gajendra served with a parachute regiment, deployed to Macedonia, and did four tours in Afghanistan, tasked with frontline peace enforcement, the security of NGOs, as well as holding instructor and mentoring roles. He retired in 2012 and now works as a manager in the security sector in the UK. He also wants to become involved in social work for military veterans. Although currently living in the UK, he feels it is important to expose his two children to both British and Nepalese culture. Gajendra was described by one of his former officers as the archetypal 'Gentleman Gurkha'.

Rifleman Chamar Bahadur Gurung, recruited in India in 1940, was deployed to the Malayan war immediately after basic training. Three battalions were captured during the conflict, including Chamar's, and the prisoners were taken to a POW camp in Singapore where they endured sleep deprivation, hard labour and frequent beatings. Chamar had to watch his brother, also a Gurkha and interned in the same POW camp, die of tuberculosis during his captivity. After he was freed, Chamar returned home to Nepal and, despite his parents' insistence that he quit, he returned to serve after three months. Upon retirement, he became a farmer. Decades later, after his wife had died and his children were no longer able to care for him, he moved into a residential home in the Kaski district of west Nepal.

Rifleman Amar Bahadur Ale grew up in Ilam, east Nepal. His father was too poor to be able to bring him up properly, so decided to marry him off at a young age. Amar was taken to the Gurkha selection in Darjeeling in 1957, when he was eighteen. By that time he had already been married for seven years and had a four-year-old child to look after. Amar had many close calls during his service, surviving a serious car accident, a landslide and a near drowning. He went on to fight in the Malayan insurgency and served in Borneo as an assistant medic. His military record of service describes him as having been extremely kind and gentle to the injured soldiers he was tasked to care for. He returned to Nepal after retiring from the Gurkhas, but now lives in the UK.

LEFT Lieutenant Manjung Gurung is ninety-four years old and almost blind. He joined the Gurkhas in 1938 and had a very successful career that included serving as a PTI, drill sergeant and jungle warfare instructor. During the Second World War, he patrolled the border between India and Afghanistan and also spent several months in Japan in a peacekeeping capacity. He was promoted to the rank of Lieutenant in 1958. Manjung went on to fight in the Malayan jungle for ten whole years against communist insurgents; he killed two high-ranking guerrillas during that time, an experience that affects him deeply to this day – he still remembers their names.

ABOVE Sapper Thamansing Gurung joined the Gurkha Engineers in 1959. After basic training and engineering courses, Thamansing worked in mechanical transport, driving plant vehicles and building roads. He served in Brunei as a driver and camp sentry and subsequently patrolled the Hong Kong border, a task he found heartbreaking as his unit was ordered to prevent desperate border jumpers from entering Hong Kong. Thamansing struggled to find work in the early 1970s after leaving the army. He tried his luck as a bus driver in India for a while and then returned to Nepal. He now lives in the UK.

ABOVE Lieutenant Purna Bahadur Gurung grew up in the 1930s, a time when the schools in his area had been closed down. But his father still wanted him to have an education and paid someone privately to teach him how to read and write. When the Second World War broke out and all the men went off to fight, he was the only one in his village who was literate, so he went round to the houses of all his neighbours to help them write to the soldiers fighting on the front lines. When the often very emotional responses arrived in the mail, he went from house to house again with a stack of letters, reading them out to the families. He was twelve years old. Purna was recruited into the British Army in 1948. He fought in the Malayan jungle, Borneo and Brunei, was awarded a Mention in Dispatches and retired a Lieutenant in 1966 after a long and successful service career. He has since worked in India, Saudi Arabia and the UK, founded several charities, one of which received a Queen's Award for Voluntary Service, and is very involved in community projects.

RIGHT Staff Sergeant Dalbahadur Sahi grew up in west Nepal in extreme poverty. He remembers as a child regularly having to walk for eight days to Tibet and south Nepal to get salt and rice for his family. He joined the Indian Army in 1944 and after three years was recruited into the Gurkhas by a British officer who was impressed by his intelligence and proactive conduct. Dalbahadur rose through the ranks quickly. He served in Japan during the Second World War and also saw fierce combat in the Malayan conflict. Upon his return to base, he was informed that his wife had died back in Nepal. Heartbroken, he went home to bury her. Eventually he remarried, and retired from the army when he found out he could not take his new wife with him to his new posting. It turned out that the most exhausting fight of his life would be his struggle to find work after retirement, and trying support his wife and children on a pension of 40 rupees per month (around £2).

LEFT Corporal Sahabir Ale spent sixteen years in the British Army and retired in 1968. His memories of life as a soldier are mostly happy ones and he speaks fondly of the camaraderie among Gurkhas on exercise and operations. Being a Gurkha saved his life more than once, even after he had already retired when, during the Nepalese civil war, armed militants came to his village knocking on doors asking for food and killing those who refused them. Sahabir stood his ground and his family was left in peace.

ABOVE Rifleman Bhimbahadur Gurung joined the British Army in 1957 and served for thirteen years, mostly in Singapore and Hong Kong. He fought in the Borneo confrontation in the 1960s for two years straight. The main thing on his mind during that time was his wife, who was waiting for him at home. Apparently it had taken a lot of convincing for his unimpressed bride to accept his proposal, even though he was a Gurkha. They are still together, having been happily married for fifty-four years, and now live in the UK.

Sapper Ghanendra Limbu was recruited in 1978 and joined the QGE after basic and engineering training. In 1982, his unit was flown to Ascension Island, roughly halfway between South America and Africa, and then shipped to the Falklands Islands at the beginning of the war between Great Britain and Argentina. Ghanendra was part of a bomb disposal team. On one occasion, while he was trying to clear a surface-to-air missile, it exploded. He lost an eye and suffered severe injuries to both hands. He was evacuated to the UK and received treatment and a subsequent medical discharge from the army. He did not receive compensation, however, and struggled to find work for a long time, desperately missing his calling as a Gurkha.

Rifleman Tek Bahadur Chhetri grew up in the Gulmi district of west Nepal and had to do hard manual labour as a child – he ploughed fields, cut grass, chopped and carried wood and tended to his family's cows. He enlisted in 1948 and served as a gunner in the Malayan war. Tek described his combat experience as three years of constant fighting and hiding, a daily back and forth of attack and retreat. He was an only child and left the army after a few years to take care of his parents. He now lives by himself in a retirement home in west Nepal, having lost all contact with his children. His grandson's wife is the only relative who still occasionally comes to visit.

ABOVE WO2 Indra Thapa, recruited in 1951, served in the Gurkha infantry as well as the Military Police. He was well educated and initially worked as a registration clerk during the Malayan war, then retrained as a military policeman, capturing enemy paratroopers and escorting them to prison camps. He is well travelled and speaks very good English due to several postings in the UK and Germany. He saw combat in Brunei and led an extensive and complex internal investigation into a mutiny during that conflict. After his MP unit disbanded, he became a dog handler, a job he loved, for the 5 Gurkha Dog Company, a short-lived outfit created in 1962 and dissolved again in 1964. He retired as a WO2 that year and bought a poultry farm in Nepal. He is still incredibly proud of being a Gurkha, calling it the Everest of careers.

RIGHT Lance Corporal Bhaluman Rai was recruited in India in 1943, far away from his native village in east Nepal. Right after completing basic training, he spent two years fighting in Burma and four more in combat in the Malayan jungle. Bhaluman's memories from both tours are still very vivid – he can recall in great detail crossing Burma's fateful Sittang Bridge with his unit while under heavy fire, losing many men whose bodies were never recovered. At one point he had to throw himself on a colleague who, suffering from severe combat stress, had started running towards enemy fire, and then pulled him to safety. Bhaluman left the army of his own accord in 1952 and returned to Nepal where he became a farmer. He has since moved to the UK.

ACKNOWLEDGEMENTS

It all started with Ken. I was in the middle of a (still ongoing) project on global law enforcement, spending a lot of time with the Sandy Springs Police Department in Georgia. That encounter led to the current Chief of Police, Ken DeSimone, agreeing to host me in his capacity as US Marine Colonel (reserves) when he was deployed to Helmand Province, Afghanistan in order to mentor the Afghan National Police. I had just suffered a string of professional and personal disappointments and was feeling defiant and a little bit brave.

Armed with naïve courage, as well as a helmet and Kevlar vest borrowed from a sympathetic law enforcement agency, I ended up in Helmand Province in the autumn of 2011. I went on patrols and police checkpoint visits with my US Marine unit every day, and tried to sort out some very conflicting feelings: my empathy for the individual soldiers I had befriended and the compassion I felt for the local population suffering under yet another decade of continuous warfare, all the while trying to get used to the daily threat of insurgent attacks and IEDs.

One night at Lashkar Gah camp, I met Lt. Col. Fraser Rea, then Commanding Officer of a Gurkha infantry regiment based there: the 2 Royal Gurkha Rifles. He asked about my police project and spontaneously invited me to accompany the Gurkhas on their mentoring trips and patrols. I immediately accepted. Having lived in the UK, I was aware of the Gurkhas and their fearsome reputation, but had never met one.

The British Army staff subsequently took it upon themselves to set up a variety of ride-alongs and stays at Gurkha patrol bases even though I wasn't an official media representative or on the list of scheduled visitors of the British Army. They were incredibly nice and generous, and went out of their way to introduce me to the Gurkhas and the work they were doing.

The Gurkhas I encountered were all soldiers from 2 RGR and mostly from B Company, which was led by their Officer in Command, Major Jamie Murray. They welcomed me with an astonishing amount of hospitality, kindness and curiosity, and I was bowled over by the unexpected gentleness and sense of humour displayed by these legendary warriors, as well as being completely fascinated by their stories: tales from Nepal, Gurkha recruitment, family life and combat.

I was wholeheartedly encouraged by Major Murray as well as Lt. Col. Rea, who suggested that I document the career arc of a Gurkha soldier (which is where the title of the book eventually came from). I realised fairly quickly that my mind was already made up – I had to do a project on the Gurkhas.

Having returned to Austria and researched existing Gurkha literature, I found that virtually all of it consisted of military history or combat anecdotes, mostly written by British Commanding Officers of Gurkha battalions. But I couldn't find much about individual Gurkhas. I wanted to portray the Gurkha soldiers themselves and offer a glimpse of their personal lives, diverse characters and backgrounds. The then Colonel of the Brigade of Gurkhas, Ian Rigden, a very generous supporter of the idea from day one, and a dispenser of sage advice and kindly pep talks later on in the project, got the ball rolling. Soon after, I found myself preparing for my first overseas exercise with 2 RGR to the jungles of Brunei. Knowing that I had to get very fit very fast, I remembered an insane-looking workout regimen the US Marines in Helmand put themselves through every day until they literally passed out – CrossFit – which consisted of Olympic weightlifting, pull-ups, push-ups, sit-ups, sprints, burpees, rowing and a variety of seemingly bizarre activities like flipping tractor tyres and hitting rubber bases repeatedly with large hammers.

I talked to the owner and head coach of Vienna's first CrossFit gym, Sebastian Rieder, and he was so enthusiastic about my project that he agreed to train me. And then, knowing about my lack of funding, he did something I will never forget – he trained me for free. For the duration of my project, Sebastian and his coaches at CrossFit Vienna and additionally Stefan Pecnik at CrossFit Graz, welcomed me into their world and coached me out of the goodness of their hearts. Having gone through a personal tragedy at the same time, CrossFit saved my sanity as well as my physical fitness and gave me the ability to survive the absurdly tough tactical exercises with the Gurkhas in Australia, Kenya and all over the UK that followed the jungle excursion.

My second sponsor appeared in the shape of a British ex-Gurkha officer named Tristan Forster, now CEO of an ethical recruitment company in Dubai called FSI Worldwide. FSI helps find work for former Gurkha soldiers and at the same time runs several charities fighting human trafficking and modern-day slavery. Tristan and his company supported the project financially, organised and paid for a significant part of my journey and hosted me for a week in Dubai. Tristan and his assistant Lucy were also very generous with moral support and daily affirmations – very underestimated but essential gifts.

And then my main sponsor showed up. CrossFit Inc., the company behind the sport I had fallen in love with, and its CEO Greg Glassman, saw something in my work that spoke to them – and they proceeded to bet on the dark horse. Without their financial support, I would have had to put the entire thing on hold halfway through.

The guys at CrossFit Inc. displayed an immediate and genuine belief in my project that never wavered, demonstrated by the occasional warm, easygoing messages from Sevan Matossian and Hayley Parlen at the company's head office. They enabled me to continue working and travelling all over the world, spending time with all the Gurkha regiments, documenting the regional and final selections in Nepal and interviewing a great number of incredible individuals, many of them unaccustomed to speaking about their personal lives, whose stories humbled me and routinely broke my heart.

Along the way, I also found out that I had the most generous and kind of friends – people like Maria, Peter and Uschi, who lent me ridiculous amounts of money and didn't care when I would pay them back; my friend Andrea, who turned into some kind of fairy godmother; Aoife and her family, who welcomed me and my horrible flu into their home in Brisbane on very short notice, despite not having seen me in fourteen years. There were also Nina, Shari, Doris, Prithvi, Lorenz, Ingeborg, Nicola, Katharina, James A., Will C., Mr, Mrs and Alex Sova in Vienna, and Biswanath-Saheb Rai and his family in Kathmandu, who not only let me house-sit their apartments, sleep on their couches and in their guestrooms, but also, without even blinking, cooked and bought me food (and drinks) on a regular basis. Then there is Eva, who lent me a backpack that got ruined in Afghanistan and took me three years to replace, as well as Wolfgang and Jackie who created the videos for my two online fundraising campaigns, an enormous amount of work I was too tech-ignorant to do myself, and Naresh, Basanta, Prithvi and Rabin, who went door to door raising money to help fund my book.

While I was spending time with Gurkhas, I tried and failed horribly at teaching myself Nepali. It wasn't an obstacle during most of the interviews because Gurkhas speak English very well, but when I sat with elderly veterans, it was a problem. So people like Yam Sunuwar of QOGLR in Aldershot, the entire staff at the Kaski Welfare Office in Nepal and Captain Mahendra and his staff of the Gurkha Welfare Advice Centre in the UK all took time out of their busy days not just to set up meetings but also to translate for me. Major Prem Ale from QG Signals spent a considerable amount of time teaching me the basics of the language, even giving me homework, something I am extremely grateful for.

There are countless individuals who were in my corner offering equipment, time, friendship, gifts and sometimes just kind words and encouragement and who are too numerous to mention. You all know who you are.

I am indebted to the many generous people who donated money to the project, in particular Jeremy Brade, Graham Thornton, *Die Weltwoche* magazine, which was the first media publication to take a serious interest in my project and whose journalist Urs Gehriger produced a wonderful eight-page article in their magazine, to Steve Reuscher for getting me my film material, and, of course, to my fantastic photo lab – the angels who developed (and often rescued) my negatives – the singularly amazing Cyberlab in Vienna and its owner, Gerhard Hinterleitner.

I am grateful to John Caine for introducing me to my publisher and a number of other supporters. Also to Charles Heath-Saunders at the Ministry of Defence and the staff at Headquarters of the Brigade of Gurkhas; the Gurkha soldiers, as well as the British Officers, OCs and Gurkha Majors, of 1 RGR, 2 RGR, particularly B Company, QGE, QG Signals, QOGLR, the Brigade Band, GSPS, Mandalay Company, Sittang Company, Gurkha Company Catterick, BGN and BGP, particularly Colonel Seán Harris; and the serving and retired Gurkhas who took the time to sit down with me and who shared their life stories, opinions and sometimes very painful experiences.

I want to thank from the bottom of my heart Natascha Auenhammer and her Zebra Labor in Vienna for developments and those stunning fine art prints, Carl Schulze for the beautiful picture on page 14, the magical 25Hours Hotel and Fanny Holzer-Luschnig for generously granting me occasional asylum, David Charters and of course Lorne Forsyth at Elliott and Thompson, my publishers. Karin Fremer, Jennie Condell, Pippa Crane of E&T – you made what only existed in my head for three years a reality. Thank you for your creativity and patience.

Gavin Edgerley-Harris at the Gurkha Museum, Winchester, for your wisdom and generosity and for letting me use some of the archived images of Gurkhas.

Lincoln and Michael at the Seven Stars Pub in Bottlesford, Wiltshire, for being a shelter on dark days.

And finally, Philip. My brother and best friend. Who talked me off the floor countless times and kept me sane.

INDEX

ABOUT THE AUTHOR

Alex Schlacher is an Austrian photographer who has done extensive work with police and military units in the US and Europe. While embedded with the US Marines in Helmand Province, Afghanistan, in 2011, she also had the privilege of spending some time with the Royal Gurkha Rifles – going on patrols with them, staying in their camps, getting to know them – and came away fascinated and in awe of their spirit, culture and dignity. She has been in the unique position of being allowed total and unprecedented access to the Brigade of Gurkhas, and has photographed them for nearly three years.

There are Gurkhas in the British Army, the Indian Army and the Singapore Police, as well as a Gurkha Reserve Unit (GRU) in Brunei.

To date, the Indian Army employs around 40,000 Gurkhas, the Singapore Police has a Gurkha Contingent of about 2,500 and the GRU is roughly 2,000-strong. This book focuses on Gurkhas of the British Army only – currently 2,500 in number.

Including the Indian Army, GRU and Singapore Police Gurkhas would have increased the size of this project beyond a manageable degree – they all deserve their own separate books.